Armstrong's Last Goodnight

AN EXERCISE IN DIPLOMACY

John Arden

EYRE METHUEN
LONDON

First published by Methuen & Co Ltd 1965
Reprinted 1970

First published as a paperback 1965
Reprinted 1966 and 1970
Reprinted 1976 by Eyre Methuen Ltd
11 New Fetter Lane, London EC4P 4EE
ISBN 0413 34370 7

© 1965, 1966 by John Arden
Printed in Great Britain by
Whitstable Litho Ltd. Whitstable Kent.

General Notes

This play is founded upon history: but it is not to be read as an accurate chronicle. The biggest liberty I have taken with the known historical facts is in connecting Sir David Lindsay with the events leading up to the execution of Johnny Armstrong in 1530. But these events must have involved considerable political and diplomatic manœuvring, and it is known that Lindsay was not only the author of *The Three Estates* and Lord Lyon King of Arms but also regularly employed upon diplomatic missions for the Scottish Crown. His own views upon the Armstrong business may be partly deduced from the lines in *The Three Estates*, where he makes his crooked Pardoner offer for sale as a blessed relic –

> . . . ane cord, baith gret and lang,
> Quhilk hangit Johne the Armistrang
> Of gude hemp, soft and sound;
> Gude, halie pepill I stand for'd
> Quha ever beis hangit with this cord
> Neidis never to be dround.

Also, in *Complaint of the Common-weal of Scotland* he says, of the state of the Border counties:

> In to the South, allace ! I was neir slane;
> Ouer all the land I culd fynd no relief:
> Almost betuix the Mers and Lowmabane
> I culd nocht knaw ane leill man be ane theif.
> To schaw thair reif, thift, murthour, and mischief,
> And vicious workis, it wald infect the air:
> And as langsum to me, for tyll declair.

From which we may guess that (*a*) he was able some years later to regard the celebrated hanging with sardonic and perhaps complacent detachment, and that (*b*) he by no means approved of the violent activities of the Border freebooters, who have in succeeding centuries found their own romantic advocates.

It is only fair to state, however, that there is – as far as I can discover – no evidence at all that Lindsay had anything whatever to do with James the Fifth's punitive expedition of 1530.

I have also made rather free with the date of the Reformation. English heresy was not likely to have been worrying the Church in Scotland at this date, and it is still less likely that any forerunners of John Knox were wandering the Ettrick Forest. But Lindsay himself took what might perhaps be called a Radical-Conservative view upon religious questions: and certain modern parallels prompted me to introduce these views into the play and to present a more extreme philosophy in the person of the Evangelist.

I have no idea whether or not Lindsay had a mistress.

In writing this play I have been somewhat influenced by Conor Cruise O'Brien's book *To Katanga and Back:* but I would not have it thought that I have in any way composed a 'Roman à clef'. The characters and episodes in the play are not based upon originals from the Congo conflict; all I have done is to suggest here and there a basic similarity of moral, rather than political, economic or racial problems.

The language of the play offered certain difficulties. It would clearly be silly to reconstruct the exact Scots speech of the period – as quoted in the two passages from Lindsay's work given above. But on the other hand, Scots was at this time a quite distinct dialect, if not a different language, and to write the play in 'English' would be to lose the flavour of the age. The Scots employed by modern poets such as MacDiarmid and Goodsir Smith owes a great deal to Lindsay, Dunbar, Henryson and the other writers of the late Middle Ages and early Renaissance: but it is also a language for the expression of twentieth-century concepts. In the end I have put together a sort of Babylonish dialect that will, I hope, prove practical on the stage and will yet suggest the sixteenth century. My model in this was Arthur Miller's adaptation of early American speech in *The Crucible*.

Note on Sets and Costumes

The play is intended to be played within the medieval convention of 'simultaneous mansions'. These are three in number and represent the Castle (for the Armstrongs), the Palace (for the Court) and the Forest (for the wild land of the Borders). The Castle and the Palace are practicable buildings, one on either side of the stage, each with a roof from which actors may speak. They need not be more than porches or tabernacles: but their style should be definite and suggestive. The Castle is a rough stone building, with battlements and a defended gate or doorway: the Palace is a more elaborate structure in the

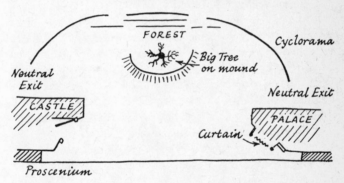

SKETCH PLAN OF SUGGESTED STAGE ARRANGEMENT

The Forest may be painted all round the Cyclorama: or else only in the centre, and the sides of the stage surround painted a neutral colour. Wherever in the course of the play a character enters or leaves the stage without it being specified that he does so via one of the three 'mansions', the Neutral Exits shewn on the sketch are intended to be employed. If there is room, space may be left between the Castle and the Palace, and the inner side of the Proscenium Arch, and this space used for entrances and exits via these two 'mansions' when several characters are involved and there is risk of overcrowding the doors of the 'buildings'. As the 'simultaneous' staging is a medieval device, and extremely formal in its conception, a formality of style should be adopted in the painting and design of the 'mansions'. If they are too naturalistic, the production will appear incongruous and peculiar.

fanciful Scots manner of Linlithgow Palace or Roslyn Chapel, painted and gilded, and topped with pretty finials. The entry is closed with a curtain, which should be painted to resemble tapestry. The Forest, which occupies the central upstage area, is basically a clump of trees. These should be dense enough to afford at least two concealed entrances for the actors: and one large tree (which should be practicable) stands in front, to the centre, and can be raised on a small mound.

The costumes should be 'working dress' – that is to say, each of the characters should be immediately recognizable as a member of his respective social class, rather than as a pictur-esque element in a colourful historical pageant. The borderers will wear mostly leather and hodden grey: the Politicians (Clerks, Commissioners, Secretaries, etc.) will be in subfusc gowns, with perhaps some use of small heraldic badges to indicate their local alignments. Lindsay wears a non-committal black suit, and adds to this at different times his herald's tabard, his scarlet robe of office, and a leather coat like Arm-strong's. The King is first seen in full regalia like an old MS. illumination. Later he appears in Highland dress for hunting. This Highland dress (and that of the Soldiers in the same scene) belongs to a period prior to the introduction of clan tartans, and its basis is the long saffron shirt – sometimes worn with a short waistcoat. The Soldiers should have bare legs and bare heads, and are armed with claymores and targets: the King could be more 'civilized' and wear hose, embroidery upon his waistcoat, and a plain bonnet. When Gilnockie dresses up in the last act he puts on an assortment of clothes obtained in raids, and they do not necessarily agree very well with each other. But his general appearance must be extremely gaudy and peacock-like. The Evangelist should wear a very plain suit of cheap material, becoming threadbare. The Cardi-nal's Secretary has the Dominican habit of black and white.

The bagpipes are, of course, lowland pipes, which were not a specifically Scots instrument at this time, but played fairly generally throughout Western Europe – c.f. the paintings of Dürer and Breughel.

Notes on the Characters

THE KING He is only seventeen, and small. He appears young for his age, and when dressed in his regalia looks like a sacred doll.

LINDSAY In his late forties, but quick and athletic in his movements, and sprightly in his speech.

MCGLASS Young, ardent, and handsome.

THE LADY Aged about thirty-five: strong, sensual, and humorous.

THE MAID Like her mistress, but slighter in body and fifteen years younger.

GILNOCKIE A great bull, or lion, of a man: he has difficulty in talking coherently, a congenital defect like an exaggerated stammer that he is only able to overcome when extremely excited or when he sings. Full of a certain innocence of spirit. Aged about forty.

GILNOCKIE'S WIFE A nervous, chaste lady, in great fear both of and for her husband.

THE ARMSTRONGS Tough loyal clansmen, devoted to their Laird. The GIRLS are their younger relatives and do the work in the house and fields. (Gentry, not peasants.)

STOBS A bitter, hard, rigid, cruel man.

YOUNG STOBS As harsh as his father, but more impulsive.

MEG Throughout the play she is shocked with grief; but before the death of her lover she has been warm, gentle, and quiet.

WAMPHRAY   A foolish handsome man, middle-aged, tough and rude-mannered. *yellow hair*

THE EVANGELIST   Aged about thirty, prematurely grey hair: a converted sensualist, his rigidity derives as much from inward doubt as from strength of character.

THE COMMISSIONERS   Experienced political gentlemen, whose emotional public remarks bear little relation to their real feelings.

THE CLERKS   They appear to be both older and wiser than their Commissioners: but, in fact, the two types are designed to work together as a team.

THE SECRETARIES   These men are really responsible for the political decisions and policies of their masters, and know it.

THE PORTER   A pompous mouthpiece, and that is all we know of him.

THE HIGHLAND CAPTAIN   Speaks with the unexpected politeness and gentleness of the Gaelic soldier. He and his men look, and no doubt fight, like wild animals.

Notes on the Casting

There are thirty parts in this play, but it may be played by a company of sixteen, if seven of the actors take more than one part, as follows:

I   FIRST SCOTS COMMISSIONER
    SECOND ARMSTRONG
    CARDINAL'S SECRETARY
II FIRST HIGHLAND SOLDIER
    SECOND SCOTS COMMISSIONER
    STOBS
    LORD JOHNSTONE'S SECRETARY

III   FIRST ENGLISH COMMISSIONER
      FIRST ARMSTRONG
IV   SECOND ENGLISH COMMISSIONER
      THIRD ARMSTRONG
      LORD MAXWELL'S SECRETARY
 V   SCOTS CLERK
      YOUNG STOBS
      PORTER
      HIGHLAND CAPTAIN
VI   ENGLISH CLERK
      KING
VII   WAMPHRAY
      EVANGELIST
      SECOND HIGHLAND SOLDIER

The remaining roles (including all the female parts) cannot conveniently be doubled. At a pinch, the GIRLS could be omitted entirely. The parts of the KING and the THIRD ARMSTRONG perhaps present problems if the respective actors have other parts to play: because it may be thought that the KING should, in order to produce a better effect in the last act, be as it were isolated: and I have suggested that the THIRD ARMSTRONG should be the Piper: in which case he may be a specialist and not necessarily a versatile actor. But this is a matter for local circumstances and taste to determine.

PS.   Also at a pinch, but may I hope only a very sharp one, two of the COMMISSIONERS may also be omitted – one from each country.

Note on Production

For the production of this play by the National Theatre at the Old Vic (1965) it was found useful to begin Act One with Scenes Three and Four, followed by Scenes One, Two and

Five. This was done in order to make an English audience familiar with the language before the more complex exposition of the plot had to be embarked upon. (Wamphray's death is an episode which more or less explains itself in visual terms, whereas the conference scene has to be *verbally* understood or it makes no sense.) I think this readjustment of scenes justified itself, and producers who wish to use it may do so: but from the point of view of the overall shape of the play, I prefer my original arrangement, which is accordingly printed here.

John Arden

Armstrong's Last Goodnight

Armstrong's Last Goodnight was first performed at the Glasgow Citizens' Theatre on 5 May 1964, with the following cast:

JAMES THE FIFTH OF SCOTLAND	Hamish Wilson
SIR DAVID LINDSAY OF THE MOUNT	Leonard Maguire
ALEXANDER MCGLASS, his Secretary	John Cairney
A LADY, Lindsay's Mistress	Lisa Daniely
HER MAID	Hannah Gordon
FIRST SCOTS COMMISSIONER	Phil McCall
SECOND SCOTS COMMISSIONER	Ian McNaughton
FIRST ENGLISH COMMISSIONER	Brian Ellis
SECOND ENGLISH COMMISSIONER	Glen Williams
CLERK TO THE SCOTS COMMISSIONERS	Alec Monteath
CLERK TO THE ENGLISH COMMISSIONERS	Stephen MacDonald
THE POLITICAL SECRETARY TO LORD JOHNSTONE	Phil McCall
THE POLITICAL SECRETARY TO LORD MAXWELL	Brown Derby
THE POLITICAL SECRETARY TO THE CARDINAL OF ST ANDREWS	Glenn Williams
PORTER TO THE ROYAL HOUSEHOLD	Alec Monteath
CAPTAIN OF THE HIGHLAND INFANTRY	Stephen MacDonald
SOLDIERS	Bill Henderson
	Peter Gordon Smith
	Brian Ellis
	James McCreadie, Jnr.
	David Gloag
	Ian Sharp
	Thomas McNamara
JOHN ARMSTRONG OF GILNOCKIE	Iain Cuthbertson
HIS WIFE — *née Janet Eliot*	Janet Michael
WILLIE ARMSTRONG	William McAllister
TAM ARMSTRONG	Alex McCrindle
ARCHIE ARMSTRONG	Alistair Colledge
FIRST GIRL OF GILNOCKIE'S HOUSEHOLD	Bonita Beach

4 Gilknockie females.

4 minstrels. – in keeping with Armstrongs.

SECOND GIRL OF GILNOCKIE'S HOUSEHOLD
                                    Aileen Salmon
THIRD GIRL OF GILNOCKIE'S HOUSEHOLD
                                    Wieslawa Kwasniewska
PIPER   Jimmy Wilson
GILBERT ELIOT OF STOBS   Harry Walker
MARTIN ELIOT, his son   Bill Henderson
MEG ELIOT, Stobs's Daughter   Anne Kristen
JAMES JOHNSTONE OF WAMPHRAY   Brown Derby
A PROTESTANT EVANGELIST   Ian McNaughton

Directed by Denis Carey
Designed by Juanita Waterson

The action of the play takes place in Scotland, early in the
second quarter of the sixteenth century.

4 minstrels.

Act One

[LINDSAY, ENGLISH *and* SCOTS COMMISSIONERS, *their* CLERKS.]

A trestle table in the middle of the stage, arranged with papers and ink etc., and stools placed for a conference.
LINDSAY (*in his herald's tabard*) *enters.*

LINDSAY. There was held, at Berwick-upon-Tweed, in the fifteenth year of the reign of James the Fift, by the Grace of God King of Scotland, and in the nineteenth year of Henry the Eight, by the Grace of God King of England, ane grave conference and consultation betwixt Lords Commissioner frae baith the realms, anent the lang peril of warfare that trublit they twa sovereigns and the leige peoples thereunto appertainen. The intent bean, to conclude this said peril and to secure ane certain time of peace, prosperity, and bliss on ilk side of the Border. I am Lord Lyon King of Arms, Chief Herald of the Kingdom of Scotland. It is my function in this place to attend upon the deliberations of the Scots Commissioners and to fulfil their sage purposes with obedience and dispatch. As ye will observe: when peace is under consideration, there is but little equability of discourse. The conference this day bean in the third week of its proceeden.

LINDSAY retires into the Palace, and immediately appears upon the roof, from which he watches the rest of the scene.
The two SCOTS COMMISSIONERS *enter from the Palace* (LINDSAY *stands aside and bows to let them pass*) *and take their seats. With them is their* CLERK.
There is a pause.

Then the ENGLISH CLERK *comes in, bows to the* SCOTS, *and takes his seat. He is followed by the* FIRST ENGLISH COMMISSIONER, *who bows and takes his seat.*
Another pause.
Enter SECOND ENGLISH COMMISSIONER; *he bows, sits, and then stands.*

SECOND ENGLISH COMMISSIONER. My lords: many weighty questions have been brought these weeks beneath discussion, and I think I may say that at least a partial agreement has been arrived at. The line of succession to the Scottish royal house; excise due upon merchandise imported or exported; claims arising from damages inflicted during previous hostilities – all these are satisfactorily settled.

FIRST ENGLISH COMMISSIONER. Heresy—

SECOND ENGLISH COMMISSIONER. Yes. The prevention and deterrence of subversive transportation of professors of alleged heresy between the realms. In the present disturbed state of Christendom, clearly we must—

FIRST SCOTS COMMISSIONER. The religious intentions of King Henry are as yet some whit ambiguous. Can he offer ane precise definition of what he means by heresy? The Court of Consistory at Sanct Andrews will desire—

FIRST ENGLISH COMMISSIONER. We have an annotation in the margin to that effect, sir. In God's Name let us not confound our business in the quagmires of theological dialectic.

SECOND SCOTS COMMISSIONER. We'll be here while neist year's harvest else. Gang forwarts, gif ye please, sir.

SECOND ENGLISH COMMISSIONER. Very well, we now come to a crucial and exceedingly delicate matter, which both parties have, I believe, agreed to leave until the last. I mean, the Security of the Borders. Or rather, their present in-security. Indeed, lords, their present state of bleeding anarchy and murderous rapine – to use no stronger words. I do not wish to revive bitter memories of past destruction. But I must remind you, lords, that the very accession to the throne of His Grace King James was consequent upon—

SECOND SCOTS COMMISSIONER. It was consequent upon the death of his father at the Field of Flodden, sir: and we're all very weel acquent with it.

SECOND ENGLISH COMMISSIONER. And how terrible was that battle. It appears to me that Scotland is not yet recovered from it. And no man here can desire its repetition.

SECOND SCOTS COMMISSIONER. Were it repeatit, it could weel find ane different conclusion. Scotland was ane dis-unitit kingdom that unlucky tide.

FIRST SCOTS COMMISSIONER. I think we have little need of historical recapitulation here. Sir, I will anticipate your argument. Ye are about to denounce the raiden and ridens of our bold Scots borderers, are ye nocht? Ye hae lost upon the English side ower mony cattle, horses, sheep, pigs, roof-trees, byres, kirk-ornaments, tableware, personal jewellery, and the maidenheids of women. Very good. We will ack-nowledge these circumstances as regrettable. But you are here for peace – ye have tellt us so yourself.

SECOND ENGLISH COMMISSIONER. It is imperative for peace that there be no more masterless raids from Scotland into England in search of booty. Or if there be, the offenders must be punished, at the hand of Scotland's Grace, and he be seen to punish them. This has not happened, has it? There is more than a suspicion that outrages of recent years have been openly encouraged, indeed in origin set on, by great men in your kingdom—

SECOND SCOTS COMMISSIONER. Sir—

SECOND ENGLISH COMMISSIONER. And great men, sir, who stand too close to Scotland's throne.

SECOND SCOTS COMMISSIONER. I want to hear their names!

SECOND ENGLISH COMMISSIONER. It were better not, I think.

SECOND SCOTS COMMISSIONER. Aha, why nocht?

SECOND ENGLISH COMMISSIONER. I do not care to rub it deeper, sir, but—

SECOND SCOTS COMMISSIONER. There's been nae riden without good reason. For every heid of cattle the Scots hae grippit, your English carls took twelve. I have a paper here—

SECOND ENGLISH COMMISSIONER. We too are furnished, sir, with papers—

FIRST ENGLISH COMMISSIONER. Permit me for one moment.

He reads from a paper:

December the 21st, last; John Armstrong of Gilnockie and his brother Armstrong of Mangerton harried twenty miles within the English ground and burned and killed their way from Bewcastle to Haltwhistle.

January the 15th: the men of Liddesdale and Eskdale rode further yet, to Hexham, and there obtained by force five score horned beasts and drove them home under moonlight, led on this occasion by John Armstrong of Gilnockie and Gilbert Eliot of Stobs. The same John Armstrong and another Eliot – I think a Martin Eliot—

FIRST SCOTS COMMISSIONER. Aye, he's the son of Gilbert – ye seem to be correct thus far.

FIRST ENGLISH COMMISSIONER. I thank you. Martin Eliot. They set their ambush on the road between Carlisle and Brampton and held to ransom no less a traveller than the Lord Abbot of Monkwearmouth and two brethren of his cloister, threatening these holy men with abominable indignities if payment were delayed.

SECOND SCOTS COMMISSIONER. And was it?

FIRST ENGLISH COMMISSIONER. Foolishly, perhaps, it was not. Two months after that the same Armstrong of Gilnockie in confederation with – with a man called James Johnstone of Wamphray—

FIRST SCOTS COMMISSIONER. Na na, ye are in error there,

sirs: Wamphray and Gilnockie are at feud. Confederation betwixt 'em's inconceivable. Look for ane other name.

SECOND ENGLISH COMMISSIONER. The name may well be mistaken. The offence took place. Has there been offered compensation? Indeed no, there has not. Why not? I reiterate: there are great men who wink at this, and England's Grace has said it is intolerable.

FIRST ENGLISH COMMISSIONER. His very word. Be warned by it. He is an angry King.

SECOND SCOTS COMMISSIONER. God: what ane turbulence of lyen janglers is this same warld we dwell in! Ye have held this business till the end, lords, gullen us and lullen us three weeks ane front of peace, of friendship, amiable words, nae threats, nae rage, nae conflict. And now it comes! I have speirt of myself ilk day, is England turnen Christian at last? Ha, ha, we have our answer! Forbye, it craves ane starker man than you are to put this Commission in dreid. We tell you, lords – in maist severe and potent voice: nae Scottish borderer receives his chastisement until sic time as we observe ane good reciprocation. Ye nourish your ain limmer thieves in Redesdale and in Tynedale – see them hangit first, and then we'll deal with ours! There is nae mair to say. Ye are deliberately provocative, and ye intend to break this Council!

FIRST ENGLISH COMMISSIONER. Indeed sir, we do not.

SECOND SCOTS COMMISSIONER. Intend it or no, then it has had that effect. Negotiation is concludit. Be reason of your intransigence. You can tell that to England's Grace, when ye gang back barren to Windsor or to Westminster. Be sure we'll tell it plain eneuch in the Palace of Halyrood.

SECOND SCOTS COMMISSIONER *goes out,* into the Palace.

SECOND ENGLISH COMMISSIONER. I warn you, this is most unwise.

FIRST ENGLISH COMMISSIONER. England's Grace has set his heart upon this treaty. Should he find himself balked therein, we cannot answer for the consequence.

FIRST SCOTS COMMISSIONER. Aye, ye won Flodden. But ye didna win the kingdom. Nor will ye win it, by ane second cast, nor third, nor fourth, against it. We are forwarnit of your malice, lords, and we ken but owerweel whaur the blame of further war will lodge.

> FIRST SCOTS COMMISSIONER *goes out into Palace.*
> The ENGLISH COMMISSIONERS *go out.*
> LINDSAY *retires from the roof of the Palace.*

SCENE TWO

[LINDSAY, ENGLISH *and* SCOTS CLERKS.]

The CLERKS *are left behind, assembling their papers and clearing away the tables and stools.*

SCOTS CLERK. Permit me, sir, ane short and private word with you.

ENGLISH CLERK. With pleasure, sir.

SCOTS CLERK. We have heard, sir, the necessair defiances deliverit in public and publicly receivit. Now sir, for the inwart verity of the business, the whilk is writ upon nae record, but I trust will rin to England's ear directly. Are ye with me, sir?

ENGLISH CLERK. I am.

SCOTS CLERK. The matter of the unruly borderers is in nae guise easy to conclude. Their depredations in truth are as muckle towards Scotland as they are towart England, and the Liddesdale and Eskdale men are sae well entrenchit in their hills, in their strang towers of defence, that they are nocht to be howkit therefrom without grave danger to the

State and expense upon the Treasury. There are, indeed, as has been said, great men in Court at Halyrood that will assume the borderers' part against all injury, and yet upon their power King James is forcit to lean, whatever be his ain opinion of their lealty. He is ane young, but prudent King, and kens his peril. Therefore, the binden and controllen of these Armstrangs, Eliots, Maxwells, and the lave, maun find itself by sure and slow advancement; and gif God will, through policy, nocht force. Are ye with me?

ENGLISH CLERK. Can it be done? And if it can, how long will it take? King Henry is impatient.

SCOTS CLERK. King Henry maun contain his patience Christ-like, sir, and virtuous, as is his wont. But the matter is in hand. The maist ferocious of these thieves, and – I will admit to ye – the hardest to suppress, is John Armstrang of Gilnockie. King James has in his grace and wisdom ordainit ane confidential emmissair to treat furthwith with Armstrang, seek some fair means of agreement, and in the end secure baith the lealty and obedience of this dangerous free-booter.

ENGLISH CLERK. Do you think that it is possible?

SCOTS CLERK. Here is the emmissair.

LINDSAY *enters from the Palace.*

Sir David Lindsay of the Mount. If he canna dae it, there is nae man that can. Sir David, d'ye see, is ane very subtle practiser, he has been tutor to the King, is now his herald, ane very pleasurable contriver, too, of farces, ballads, allegories, and the like delights of poetry. He has wit, ye ken, music, ane man of rhetoric and discreet humanity. Do I flatter ye, Sir David, or are ye indeed serpent eneuch to entwine the Armstrangs in your coil?

LINDSAY (*to* ENGLISH CLERK). Come here, sir, here . . . Whilk man of us twae is the better dressit, d'ye think?

ENGLISH CLERK. Dressed?

LINDSAY. Aye, dress it.

ENGLISH CLERK. I scarcely understand you, sir. But if you intend a sense of correctness and decency of apparel, I do not think myself in any way at fault. My clothes express my function: unassuming, cleanly, subfusc. You, of necessity, wear your official livery, which is, of necessity, both splendid and delightful, and suited to the pageantry of state. Is that what you would have me say?

LINDSAY. Aye, it'll serve. Splendid and delightful. As it were, ane ornament for a Mayday foolery or ane heathenish idol dedicate to blood-sacrifice. I will remove it, d'you mark? There is ane man under it, and remove what's left upon him, and there's naething for ye but nakedness. What can we dae wi' that in the service of diplomacy?

> The rags and robes that we do wear
> Express the function of our life
> But the bawdy body that we bear
> Beneath them carries nocht
> But shame and greed and strife.
> It is pleisand to naebody
> Of its hairy sweat and nudity;
> Save belike to ane cruel tormentor
> Whaur his whip will leave the better bloody mark,
> Or save belike to our ain rejoict Creator,
> Whaur he walks through the green glade
> Of his fair garden and his fencit park,
> Or save belike to ane infatuate tender woman:
> And then best in the dark.
> Yet here I stand and maun contrive
> With this sole body and the brain within him
> To set myself upon ane man alive
> And turn his purposes and utterly win him.
> That coat is irrelevant:
> I will wear it nae further
> Till Armstrang be brocht

Intil the King's peace and order.
I will gang towart his house
As ane man against ane man,
And through my craft and my humanity
I will save the realm frae butchery
Gif I can, good sir, but gif I can.

ENGLISH CLERK. Is there not, however, a more certain way than that? Your Commissioner mentioned a feud between the Armstrongs of Gilnockie and, er, and—

SCOTS CLERK. Wamphray. James Johnstone of Wamphray. Aye, they are at feud.

ENGLISH CLERK. Then why not offer Wamphray, from the hand of the King, some sort of emolument – I mean, in short, give a bribe to one ruffian to do away with the other?

SCOTS CLERK. M'm, we did consider it. And Johnstone was agreeable. But the man is a greit-heidit fool: he's no killt Armstrang yet, and I canna believe he ever will. It was sheer waste of hard-gathert taxes.

LINDSAY. Mair than taxes, man – humanity. To murder ane murderer is a'thegither waste, and bad waste at that. Like silly wee childer that pick up a caterpillar – they crush it in their fingers, and then ye find them greeten ower the dearth of butterflies in summer. Besides, it's no sae simple. This caterpillar is protectit. He is the vassal of Lord Maxwell.

SCOTS CLERK (to ENGLISH CLERK). Ane tyrannous and malignant peer at the Court and ane constant threatener of rebellion. Nae Armstrang rides against England outwith his implicit permission.

LINDSAY. Or indeed occult command. The nobility of this land, sir, are mair treacherous and insensate than ony gang of thieves in Christendom . . . I wad never condemn ane proposition to murder Lord Maxwell. There are mony good poison mushrumps grow in the Ettrick forest – on my road to Gilnockie I could gather ye a wee bag, eh? Will I dae it? Wad ye like it?

SCOTS CLERK (*gives an embarrassed giggle*). Just so, Sir David, just so . . . When do you intend to ride?

LINDSAY. To Gilnockie? Directly.

SCOTS CLERK. And what people will ye bring?

LINDSAY. Aye well, there will be the lady—

SCOTS CLERK. The lady? Your wife.

LINDSAY. Did I say that? She is ane paramour, sir – aha, ye do mislike it?

SCOTS CLERK. Ah na na . . . But when all is said and done, sir, do you find her presence ane absolute necessity?

LINDSAY. Absolute. At unpredictable intervals: but absolute. (*To* ENGLISH CLERK.) Do ye remember the story of the Gordian knot?

ENGLISH CLERK. I think that I may recollect—

LINDSAY. Aye well, there was ane emperour, and he went with ane sword and cut it. He thocht he was ane god, walken. Why in God's Name could he no be a human man instead and sit down and unravel it?

SCOTS CLERK. You yourself, Sir David, are to show him the way there, I take it.

He takes him out of earshot of the ENGLISH CLERK.

And shew him it with speed, as ye hope for your salvation! Scotland can nocht sustain ane other war with England. The conference is broke, the urgency is merciless—

LINDSAY. Aye, aye, we ken . . . (*To* ENGLISH CLERK.) He says it is ane urgency. Well, Lindsay's urgent, too. Observe him: he's awa'. (*Exit into Palace.*)

ENGLISH CLERK. I will report to the Grace of England what I have been told: and I will pray for your success. Good day, sir, fare you well. (*Exit.*)

The SCOTS CLERK *stands hesitating for an instant and then goes into the Palace.*

Start of play

SCENE THREE

[GILNOCKIE, WAMPHRAY, ARMSTRONGS.]

Hunting horns, sounds of hounds and horses.
  Enter, through the Forest, GILNOCKIE *and his men, dressed for the chase.*
  WAMPHRAY *comes with them, arm in arm with* GILNOCKIE.

WAMPHRAY (*to audience*).
  To the hunten ho, cried Johnny Armstrang
  And to the hunten he has gaen
  And the man that seeks his life, James Johnstone,
  Alang with him he has him taen.

FIRST ARMSTRONG.
  To the hunten ho, cried Johnny Armstrang,
  The morning sun is on the dew,
  The cauler breeze frae aff the fells
  Will lead the dogs to the quarry true.

SECOND ARMSTRONG.
  They huntit hie, they hunted law,
  They huntit up, they huntit down,
  Until the day was past the prime
  And it grew late in the afternoon.
  They huntit hie by the Millstane Edge
  Whenas the sun was sinken law—

GILNOCKIE. Ca aff the dogs!

  This cry is taken up offstage and horns blow again.

SECOND ARMSTRONG.
  Says Johnny then, ca aff the dogs
  We'll bait our steeds and hamewart go.

  They sit down to rest.

THIRD ARMSTRONG.
  They lightit hie at the Ewes Water Heid

Between the brown and benty ground
They rested them but a little wee while:
Tak tent then lest ye sleep too sound.

FIRST ARMSTRONG. We hae gien ye but poor hunten, Wamphray. The dun deer of Eskdale had word ye were comen, I think. They're awa beyond into Teviotdale to bide on their lane there until we show them our backs.

GILNOCKIE (*passing a flask*). Tak a drink while we rest. Let the huntsmen earn their meat. Sit ye down for God's sake.

WAMPHRAY. It was ane gentlemanlike and honourable action for ye, Gilnockie, to celebrate the reconciliation betwixt our houses with this day's sport, howsoever frustratit, and a bottle of good usquebaugh. Gie ye lang life and fruitful riden.

FIRST ARMSTRONG. And the Grace of God betide us all intil ane time of peace and friendship.

GILNOCKIE. We have but few years left us, James.

FIRST ARMSTRONG. And then we maun gang to our graves. The Laird of Gilnockie wad tell ye, forbye, this reconciliation requires some formal handfast and ane apparent declaren before witnesses.

GILNOCKIE. You men, are ye with me, hear it, all you men! Your hand!

He clasps hands with WAMPHRAY *in a ceremonious fashion.*

FIRST ARMSTRONG. Neither Armstrang nor Johnstone frae this day furth shall pursue their ancient enmity. All plots, devices, ambuscades or manslauchters, either to t'ither, conceivit, intendit, or made in time past are hereby void, forgotten, and entirely outwith the consideration of our lives. In their stead stands friendship, britherhood, and ane certain protection and assistance against all heinous attempts. Is that weel spoken? Gilnockie wad be glad of your agreement.

WAMPHRAY. Under witness of God, Jesus His hangit Son, and the Haly Ghaist in Trinity, I call it weel spoken.

Johnny, God help me, I could desire ane equal word frae
Gilbert Eliot of Stobs. You are yet close confederate with
him; could ye no mak his people turn towart me in peace in
like manner with your ain?

GILNOCKIE. Gilbert Eliot? The man has ane dochter.

FIRST ARMSTRONG. It wad be nae matter of difficulty,
Wamphray, gif there were little mair than driven kye or
broken byres in dispute betwixt the Eliots and yourself. But
Gilbert believes ye hae lain wi his dochter.

GILNOCKIE. Against her will, he tells me.

WAMPHRAY. Ah na, na, na, against her will is ridiculous.

GILNOCKIE. But ye did swyve the lassie?

WAMPHRAY. Aye, that I did.

FIRST ARMSTRONG. Ye are ane free widower, however.
Gilnockie wad speir what prevents ye frae marriage.

THIRD ARMSTRONG. Ye will mind that Gilnockie's ain wife
is the sister of Stobs: ane alliance betwixt the three houses
wad be gey convenient, Wamphray.

GILNOCKIE. Convenient. Wad be honourable. Tak ye ane
other drink!

WAMPHRAY. Alliance, marriage, are ye out of your senses?
Gif I called Meg Eliot my kirkfast marriet wife, within less
than a year my ain greeten wean'd call the pigman of
Wamphray by the name of bloody uncle! Ach God, she is
ane gat-leggit strumpet, Johnny, and I tell you I kent it the
first half-hour after!

GILNOCKIE. After? What after?

WAMPHRAY. Heh heh, what d'ye think?

FIRST ARMSTRONG. Ye'll no tell that to Stobs.

WAMPHRAY. I seek nae opportunity to tell anything to Stobs.
He can find it for himself.

FIRST ARMSTRONG. Gif he finds *you*, sir, you will be finishit.
His castle is nae mair than ten miles awa frae here. Suppose
that *he* should hae chosen to hunt these fells the day? What
wad ye do?

WAMPHRAY. I wad call upon my host for assistance and protection in accordance with his word.

FIRST ARMSTRONG. Aye. Gilbert nor his sons wad never do you violence gif you were standen with the Armstrangs: there's nae question o' that. Forbye he is ane sudden man with his weapon, Gilbert; he has three and twenty notches cut in his hilt for the lives he has taen of men that were in search of his. I mind that he said to the Laird: I ha never yet heard of the laddie that wad kill me, he said, but what I was forewarnit of it and dealt him ane quick vengeance before he could sae mickle as graith up his brand.

GILNOCKIE. Speir at him what wad he do—

FIRST ARMSTRONG. He says what wad ye do, what action wad ye set afoot, gif ye heard there was ane complot made by your enemies to brenn your house aboon your heid and you in your nakit bed with your wife and your bairn, sleepen?

WAMPHRAY. Gif I heard that, I wad – I wad first demand matter of proof of it, Gilnockie.

GILNOCKIE. Aye, aha, aye?

FIRST ARMSTRONG. There was ane trustless word abroad that sic ane black design was in process upon Gilnockie, upon the safety of our castle, upon Janet the Laird's wife, upon his bairn within the cradle, upon the good men in his hall – is this the truth?

WAMPHRAY. Gilnockie, he said trustless. Trustless is true. Nae circumstance else.

GILNOCKIE. Wad ye tak aith upon that?

WAMPHRAY. What?

FIRST ARMSTRONG (*producing a book from his pouch*). Wad ye swear upon the Gospel? Ye are aware of nae plot by fire or by steel to destroy John o'Gilnockie while he sleeps?

GILNOCKIE. There's the Book, there.

FIRST ARMSTRONG. Are ye preparit to swear it, sir?

WAMPHRAY. I hae gien ye already ane handfast of friendship.

GILNOCKIE. Aye: mak it sicker. Tak aith upon the Book.

WAMPHRAY. Gilnockie. Ye do wrang. Indeed, ye do me wrang to insist upon this thing.

GILNOCKIE. Insist? Jamie, I wad never.

FIRST ARMSTRONG. Your word, sir, is your honour, and it's no to be disputit. Sit ye down with the Laird, you are his good friend. But ye ken very weel, upon this Border, a man maun look keen to his ain proper safety.

GILNOCKIE (sings).

There's nane may lean on a rotten staff
But him that risks to get a fall:
There's nane that may in a traitor trust
Yet trustit men may be traitors all.

FIRST ARMSTRONG. I assure ye, sir, they may.

GILNOCKIE. Toom the bottle, Jamie, we're nane of us fou yet.

WAMPHRAY. Nor like to be neither, on the edge-hills of Teviot. Good luck then and good horsemanship to auld Gibby of Stobs, and the reeken breeks of his dochter! He-hech—

(He sings.)

And when he came to the hie castle yett
He beat upon that door
Oh where are you, my lily-white love,
Where are you, you dirty whoor!

He gives a drunken laugh and lies back. The others do likewise, and all appear to fall asleep. When WAMPHRAY is clearly snoring heavily, the ARMSTRONGS sit cautiously up.

GILNOCKIE signs to the FIRST ARMSTRONG, who slips off into the Forest.

GILNOCKIE. Brand. Get his brand. Tangle it up.

The SECOND ARMSTRONG takes WAMPHRAY'S sword and wraps twine about the hilt, tying it to the scabbard.

Let's hae his gully-knife.

The SECOND ARMSTRONG *passes over to him* WAMPHRAY'S *knife.*

You the gun.

The THIRD ARMSTRONG *picks up* WAMPHRAY'S *handgun.*

THIRD ARMSTRONG. Loadit.

GILNOCKIE. Aye. Water.

THIRD ARMSTRONG. We've nae water here. Do ye want me to—

GILNOCKIE. Then pour in bloody usquebaugh and ask nae mair fool questions.

THIRD ARMSTRONG (*pouring whisky down the barrel*). This is no a very provident method, Gilnockie. I doubt—

GILNOCKIE. Do it.

THIRD ARMSTRONG. Aye.

GILNOCKIE (*looking at the sword*). He'll yet pull that out. See. Mak it sicker.

He improves the knots at the sword-hilt. The FIRST ARMSTRONG *returns, holding a bridle.*

FIRST ARMSTRONG. Here's his bridle.

GILNOCKIE. What hae ye done wi' the horse?

FIRST ARMSTRONG. I've whippit him hame to bloody mither.

GILNOCKIE. Good. He's still asleep.

He puts back the sword.

SECOND ARMSTRONG. Gilnockie. Are you entirely clear that this affair is in consonance with your—

GILNOCKIE. With my what?

SECOND ARMSTRONG. With your – with your honour, Gilnockie?

GILNOCKIE. What's your name?

SECOND ARMSTRONG. My name is Armstrong.

GILNOCKIE. Aye, I thocht it wad be. Then you see that you keep it.

They stand around waiting, and looking into the distance.

FIRST ARMSTRONG. A quarter hour frae now and the red sun's drappit under. Whaur to hell are the Eliots?

A horn in the distance.

Ah: here they are. It should be Gilbert the Laird and his eldest son, aye riden like a pair of wildwood bogles! (*He speaks to the sleeping* WAMPHRAY.) James Johnstone of Wamphray, ye are ane sackless murderit man.

GILNOCKIE. Wake him up: wi' that.

The THIRD ARMSTRONG *blows a horn in* WAMPHRAY'S *ear.*

WAMPHRAY (*starts up*). Eh, who, what—

FIRST ARMSTRONG. Wamphray, we're trappit. There's fifteen of the Eliots riden ower the north rigg. Mount your steed, man, and gang!

WAMPHRAY. Eh, what, gang whaur?

FIRST ARMSTRONG. Back to Gilnockie's castle; they are riden at feud!

GILNOCKIE. Get to your horses!

His men run out into the Forest.

Come on, man, awa—

WAMPHRAY. Johnny, whaur's my horse?

GILNOCKIE *runs out after his men.*

FIRST ARMSTRONG (*off*). Awa hame to bloody mither!

THIRD ARMSTRONG (*off*). Wamphray, ye are ane forsworn traitor, and ye maun bide there for what comes after ye!

Their laughter is heard receding, off.

SCENE FOUR

[WAMPHRAY, STOBS, YOUNG STOBS, MEG.]

WAMPHRAY *looks around him in despair.*

WAMPHRAY. Bide here for what – fifteen men, fifteen Eliots, on their horses, at feud— (*He tries to draw his sword.*) The kindless bastard! (*He looks around and picks up his gun.*) And what's he done to the gun? Sodden, sodden weet and cloggit wi' usquebaugh – why, the gun's fou! Jamie's fou, too . . . Gully, gully, he's not even left me my gully-knife, gin he'd left me but that I could cut free my brand—

He sits down helplessly, tugging at the knots on his hilt.

STOBS (*off*). Johnstone?

YOUNG STOBS (*off*). Johnstone of Wamphray.

STOBS (*off*). Are ye there, my mannie, are ye there?

YOUNG STOBS (*off*). We're here.

STOBS (*off*). We want ye.

STOBS *and* YOUNG STOBS *enter from the Forest. They carry hunting spears.*

Wamphray. Ye ken our names and ye ken our quarrel. There is auld feud betwixt us lang syne, Wamphray, and this month it is augmentit. Ye hae lain leg across my dochter and we're here to kill ye for it. Will ye stand to your death like a man, or will ye squat upon your hurdies like a wee doggie wi' the worms?

He pricks him with his spear and WAMPHRAY *jumps up and back. He holds his scabbarded sword on guard in front of him.*

YOUNG STOBS. That brand's little good to ye, gif Gilnockie kent his business.

WAMPHRAY *fights them hopelessly, using his sword as though it were a cudgel, but they force him back to the big tree, and pin him to it with their spears.*

WAMPHRAY. When ye neist gratify your wame at Johnny Armstrang's table, speir at him frae me, what betidit with his honour?

He dies.

STOBS. I do nocht regard this as a relevant question. Gilnockie has certain proof that this thing we hae pit down, here, was collaborate with ane undiscoverit enemy to oerthrow Gilnockie's people. And, with his people, ours. He will remain here on this fellside for the better nourishment of the corbies. Ride.

The two ELIOTS *go out through the Forest, leaving the spears in the body.*
MEG *enters at another side of the Forest. After a pause:*

MEG. Jamie? . . . Jamie? . . . Ah, they hae finisht their wark with ye, Jamie, they hae finisht it gey complete. There are nae better butchers in the land.

She pulls out the spears. The body slumps down and she kneels beside it.

In twa minutes they hae turnit ye intil ane auld man; ye werena that last week.
    These lips that were sae red and fat
    Will snarl across your chaps for ever
    Like the grin of a dirty rat:
    The yellow hair sae sleek and fine,
    That did illuminate your hard hasty skull
    And the deep secret dale here of your chine,
    In twa minutes has revertit
    To the draff-black bristles of a wild-wood swine.
    James, ye cruel drunken lecher James,
    Whaur is now departit
    Your thrust and tender carelessness of lust?
    And in what unkent bed do ye scatter

Your barren seed this nicht? Aye, totter,
Stagger, stumble intil sleep:
Nae Matthew, Mark, nor Luke, nor John, will keep
Their watch oer you—
To baith your woman and your godly faith
Ye were untrue.
Are ye comen, my wearie dearie,
Are ye comen, my lovely hinnie,
I will find ye a wee bracken bush
To keep the north wind frae aff your ancient body.

She drags the corpse out into the Forest.

SCENE FIVE

[LINDSAY, MCGLASS.]

LINDSAY *enters from the Palace.*

LINDSAY (*to audience*). The grief of this woman is the grief of the Common-weal of Scotland. Naebody to hear it, and but few to comprehend it, gif they did. And of those few, how mony could comprehend the means of consolation? Where is my secretair? Alexander? Mr McGlass!

Enter MCGLASS *from.the Palace.*

MCGLASS. Are ye ready for the road, Sir David? We had best lose nae time setten furth. God kens what could happen upon the South-West Border before we get there. They tell me there is ane manslauchter within ten mile of Carlisle every third day.

LINDSAY. I wait, Mr Alexander, for my wanton and unpunctual lady. Whaur is she, d'ye ken?

MCGLASS She was to hae left Linlithgow in good time to hae met with us on the road, but this day I have ane letter frae

Jedburgh to say that she is held there by the ill condition of the weather and that she will proceed to Gilnockie's castle on her ain when there is better chance of travel.

LINDSAY. I am of opinion, Mr Alexander, that the lady's love and inclination towart me is somewhat fainter than it did use to be. Do you imagine she will hae fand ane better man for her pastime?

MCGLASS. Better man than Lindsay? Better for what? The poetry of love or the wicked deed itself? Either gate, I think it were scarce possible.

LINDSAY. Ye have ane gey feeble notion then of the bounds of possibility. Will ye no sing ane sang as we travel?

MCGLASS. Gaelic or Scots?

LINDSAY. Scots, man: we're in the Lawlands. And mak it ane sang of the unkindness of womankind.

MCGLASS (*sings as they march with* LINDSAY *joining in the refrains.*)

> When I cam hame frae riden out
> I fand my love in bed.
> A minstrel harp hung on the rail
> And a coat of the scarlet red.
> 'What man was here?' I speirt at her
> And this is what she said –
>   'Oh a dree dree dradie drumtie dree.'
>
> 'My brither cam at mirk midnicht
> He was sae cauld and weet
> That I maun fetch him intil bed
> And warm his frozen feet.
> Indeed his feet are warm eneuch
> And his instrument sae sweet
>   Plays a dree dree dradie drumtie dree.'

LINDSAY. Aye, and it's now time to hear a bit out o' *your* instrument. Here is the castle of Gilnockie: we stand before his yetts: gie him ane blaw of the wee trump.

MCGLASS, *who carries a bugle horn, blows a blast.*

Blood and wounds, are they all deaf in there? Blaw again.

MCGLASS *blows a second call.*

SCENE SIX

[LINDSAY, MCGLASS, GILNOCKIE, *his* WIFE, ARM-
STRONGS.]

GILNOCKIE'S WIFE *appears on top of the Castle.*

GILNOCKIE'S WIFE. Who are ye? What's your business?
Frae what place d'ye come here? This is John o'Gilnockie's
castle and the Laird has nae desire for strangers. Declare
yourselves directly.

LINDSAY. Madam: I am sent here by the King.

FIRST ARMSTRONG *appears at the Castle gate.*

FIRST ARMSTRONG. And whatten King wad that be?

MCGLASS. King James of Scotland: what King d'ye think
else?

FIRST ARMSTRONG. King of Scotland? King of bloody
Lothian. That's the best name he carries here.

GILNOCKIE'S WIFE. Willie, Tam, Archie – here are men frae
the King—

Two more ARMSTRONGS *emerge from the Castle, with
weapons.*

Fasten their hands. They hae come here to wark us ane
treason.

The men seize LINDSAY *and* MCGLASS *and tie their hands
behind their backs, and take away their swords.*

FIRST ARMSTRONG. Blawen your damn trumpets before the
yetts of Gilnockie. The Laird'll hae ye hangit.

MCGLASS. Hangit!

LINDSAY. Hangit? For what indeed?

MCGLASS. We are servants of the King—

FIRST ARMSTRONG. There's but ae King in Eskdale, my mannie, and he's King John the Armstrang. We hae them fast bandit, mistress.

> GILNOCKIE'S WIFE *has left the top of the Castle and now comes out of the gate, below.*

Will we pit them in the black hole?

GILNOCKIE'S WIFE. Na, na, no yet. The Laird'll want to see them when he is risen frae his meat.

THIRD ARMSTRONG. He'll no want to see them stood like ornament statues within the width of his yard, mistress. They maun gang beneath the trap-hatches, quick.

> *The* FIRST ARMSTRONG *begins to hustle them.*

GILNOCKIE'S WIFE. Willie, let them be. I'll speak a word wi' them first.

FIRST ARMSTRONG. The Laird'll no be pleast at it.

GILNOCKIE'S WIFE. Willie.

FIRST ARMSTRONG. Whatever ye say, mistress: ye are the Laird's lady.

GILNOCKIE'S WIFE (*to the* ARMSTRONGS). Stand a bit back, sirs; remember your places.

> *They withdraw, rather sulkily.*

Tam, will ye fetch me my chair? Tam, my chair, gif ye please!

> *The* SECOND ARMSTRONG *goes into the Castle and brings out a chair.*

FIRST ARMSTRONG (*aside*). I had best to tell Gilnockie what has chancit within his house.

THIRD ARMSTRONG (*aside*). Tak tent, he will be angry.

FIRST ARMSTRONG. I had best tell him.

The FIRST ARMSTRONG *goes into the Castle.*

GILNOCKIE'S WIFE (*sitting down on the chair*). The Laird
will be angry. Ye are aware, are ye no? that the King has
had him proclaimit outlaw and rebel at Edinboro Cross and
that he in return has proclaimit the King nae King ower
Eskdale but ane traitor to his people. Frae what cause do ye
come to this border but to bring tyranny and coercion to the
inhabitours thereof? I tell ye, Gilnockie will be angry, and
when he is angry he is ane man to consider with. In God's
Name, he is ane devil, sirs – and you yourselves are ane pair
of equal devils, ye are Mephistophilis and Beelzebub, to
stir up mair warfare when there is but peace and truce here
and community in Christ.

LINDSAY. In Christ, madam? Is that the verity? Community
with the English? The English are Christian men.

GILNOCKIE'S WIFE. The Laird and his people have sufferit
mickle wrang frae the English. Ower generation and generation the English hae warkit destruction frae Carlisle to the
Ettrick Forest and frae the forest to the sea-coast, and alang
the sea-coast intil Forth. The Laird has his purposes – they
are strang purposes for defence. He has aye been courageous
in their difficult fulfilment, and what hae ye to tell him that
will serve him ony advantage, but rather cruel hurt to his
peace, and disadvantage to his people, sirs; for the Laird *is*
his people, and his people were ance the King's, but now they
are naebody's. Gilnockie is their ae protection. They maun
starf outwith his hand. What are your names?

LINDSAY. I am David Lindsay of the Mount. Ye will hae
heard of me, I guess?

GILNOCKIE'S WIFE. Fore God, ye are the King's Herald?

LINDSAY. I am. And this gentleman is Mr Alexander McGlass,
my servant and my writer.

MCGLASS. Madam, I am maist honourit to offer ye ane salutation.

GILNOCKIE'S WIFE. What? What? What honour to mock at
me in the very house of my good man, ane puir terrifyit
woman, haven ane bitter weird of violence aye thrawn within
my spirit, sir? Gilnockie will be angry. What soldiers have
ye brocht here?

LINDSAY. Nae soldiers at a', madam.

SCENE SEVEN

[LINDSAY, MCGLASS, GILNOCKIE, *his* WIFE, ARMSTRONGS
and GIRLS.]

GILNOCKIE *enters with* FIRST ARMSTRONG *from the Castle.
His* WIFE *gets up from the chair and he takes her place. He
looks keenly at the two prisoners.*

GILNOCKIE. Their names.

SECOND ARMSTRONG. Lindsay, McGlass.

GILNOCKIE. Mac – Mac – Mac – Glass? Ane Hielandman?
He wears breeks.

SECOND ARMSTRONG. He spak to us in good Scots.

GILNOCKIE. Better than that – me – the Gaelic, me. Ha ha,
how's this? Hechna, hochna, hochna, hoo! Ha ha ha—

FIRST ARMSTRONG. There is an exposition of versatility for
ye, mister; what d'ye think o' that for ane good Lawland mou
full of dirty Erse?

GILNOCKIE. Lindsay. That is ane name: I heard it. Delamont:
Lindsay of the Mount. David Lindsay Delamont. Sir.

GILNOCKIE'S WIFE. Aye, that is correct, Gilnockie, ane kent
man: Sir David Lindsay of the Mount, he is the Herald of
the King.

GILNOCKIE. Herald, King? Herald, Herod, King, the wee
childer. Ilk ane o' them murderit. Cut oot their throats.

Jesus Christ escapit. King Herod was ane King: and he doubtless had ane Herald.

FIRST ARMSTRONG. The Laird intends to tell ye, sir, that him that ye serve is but ane prodigious tyrant, like—

GILNOCKIE. Will be. God he is ane bloody wean yet.

FIRST ARMSTRONG. The Laird tells ye furthermair—

LINDSAY. The Laird can tell me himself. He has ane tongue of his ain, has he no? What for does he talk to me through varlets?

GILNOCKIE *roars*.

GILNOCKIE'S WIFE. Sir, ye had best apprehend—

FIRST ARMSTRONG. Ye had best apprehend, sir, that the Laird has had ane impediment in his speech syne the day of his nativity. He receives his interpretation through the words of his leal gentlemen.

GILNOCKIE'S WIFE. You are discourteous to remark upon it, Sir David.

GILNOCKIE. Gentlemen. That's no the women. Haud your damn't whist.

GILNOCKIE'S WIFE. I crave pardon, indeed, John, for the interruption of your discourse—

He glares at her and she is silent.

GILNOCKIE (*fingering* LINDSAY'S *clothes*). Silk. Satin. Velvet. Gowd – is it gowd?

GILNOCKIE'S WIFE. It's gilt-siller, Gilnockie. I'm no yet ane Marquess.

GILNOCKIE. Aye? No yet's Johnny.

MCGLASS. Ye could be, could ye no?

GILNOCKIE (*showing his own clothes*). See. Linsey-woolsey. Buft leather. Steel. Hackit steel. Hackit flesh. Here is ane brand. (*He draws his sword.*) She gies ye answer to her name. Tell him.

FIRST ARMSTRONG. He calls his brand Kings' Dread,

Delamont. Because that is her manner of life. Compare them.

He measures GILNOCKIE'S *sword against* LINDSAY'S.

GILNOCKIE. Langer, braider, heavier. Nae King whatever—

FIRST ARMSTRONG. Nae King whatever has had the might to put down Armstrang. Jamie Stuart the Fourth sent against us ane officer, and horsemen forbye. And hear ye what sang was made by his people – the Laird wi' his ain hand slew—

GILNOCKIE (*sings*).

> I slew the King's Lieutenant
> And garr'd his troopers flee
> My name is Johnny the Armstrang
> And wha daur meddle wi' me?

The ARMSTRONGS *pick up the refrain and repeat it.*

LINDSAY. Wha daur? David Lindsay daur. King Johnny of Eskdale indeed! King Curlew of the barren fell. King Paddock of the wowsie mosses. Ye squat on your blood-sodden molehill and ye hoot, Johnny: and naebody in Scotland considers ye mair than a wet leaf blawn against the eyeball on a day of September wind. So ye slew the King's Lieutenant, hey? And whatten reck d'ye imagine the King made of that? What hour or what wee minute was reft out of the Royal sleep, what disturbit instant was thrust in for you betwixt James Stuart and his concubine when he heard word of the peril of Gilnockie in the corner of his border? Fore God, ye have ane precellent conceit of your power, Mr Armstrang!

GILNOCKIE *growls*.

Ye are ane inconvenience, I will grant ye. Ye are ane tedious nuisance to the realm. Ye are indeed cause for ane itchy paragraph or twae in some paper of state. But were ye the great man of danger and subversion that ye fain, sir, wad think yourself, can ye credit then the King's Herald wad hae come to your house wi' nae footmen nor horse, nae pikemen nor archers, nae bombardiers nor pioneers – wi' nocht in God's Name but ane demi-priestling writer and sax inches of bent brass bugle! I crave your pardon, Sandy, I had nae intent to disparage ye, but the noise that ye mak on your instrument can scarcely be callit the clangour of warfare.

GILNOCKIE. Armstrang. Mr Armstrang. *Mister*—

FIRST ARMSTRONG. The Laird has his proper entitlement of style. He's no ashamit to use it, nor yet to hear it usit. *Gilnockie*, gif ye please, when ye open your mou to the Laird!

LINDSAY. Gilnockie, gif ye will. He draws his rent frae the local middens, by all means let us concede him the flattery of their name.

> GILNOCKIE *leaps forward and grips* LINDSAY *by the throat, shaking him in rage.*

FIRST ARMSTRONG. Will we hang him, Gilnockie?

SECOND ARMSTRONG. Cut his heid off?

THIRD ARMSTRONG. I'll dae it – this minute!

GILNOCKIE (*throwing* LINDSAY *down*). Na . . . Ane precellent conceit. Nocht, in God's Name, but ane writer and ane bugle. To stand against me. Johnny. For what?

FIRST ARMSTRONG. Aye, tell him; for what?

GILNOCKIE. Willie, search his purpose.

FIRST ARMSTRONG (*hauling* LINDSAY *upright again*). You are ane courageous man, Delamont, to heave up your undefendit face intil the face of Gilnockie. Gif you're no here for coercion, ye maun hae brocht with ye ane offer of terms. Do I pursue the passage of your mind correctly, Gilnockie?

GILNOCKIE. Aye.

FIRST ARMSTRONG. Declare to the Laird, then, first, what does the King want?

LINDSAY. He wants to prevent ane English conquest of the kingdom. For what else is he King?

GILNOCKIE (*laughs*). And is the riden – Gilnockie, Stobs, or paddock of the mosses – ride intil England, and prick them, prick them – can we – hey?

FIRST ARMSTRONG. The Laird means, Delamont, that when he and his good-brither Eliot mak ane raid intil England, the whilk ye hae just tellt us is ane insignificant provocation at the hands of unregardit men, then what way can this insignificance gar the great King of England set abroach ane formal war? Can we prick King Henry's quarters indeed thus sharply – when our lances are sae blunt, and short, and pitiable?

LINDSAY. I had nae sort of intent towart sic ane implication. Your raidens and ridens are naething of import whatever. But English policy *is*: and English policy, continual sin the time of heroic Wallace, is the domination of Scotland and the destruction of her rulers. True, or untrue?

GILNOCKIE. True.

LINDSAY. Aha, we progress. Now let us bear our minds back, a wee space intil history. I could bear mine the mair freely gif my hands were to be loosit – gesticulation, whiles, is ane useful stimulant to the deftness of the tongue—

GILNOCKIE. Na.

LINDSAY. Ah . . . Intil history. Bannockburn. Ane victory. Wha won it?

GILNOCKIE. We did.

LINDSAY. You. And the Bruce?

GILNOCKIE. The Bruce? He was nocht, was nae place, was but deid but for gentlemen. Armstrang. In that battle. There was he. Aye and Eliot. Otterburn alsweel. It was Armstrang did mak prisoner Hotspur Percy. Of this aye house the bonny gentlemen.

LINDSAY. Precise. Ane veritable conception of history indeed. It was upon sic perilous occasions that the Lawland gentlemen

alane did create the defence of this realm: when baith
monarchy and nobility were shook with internecine faction
like the bell-ropes in the tower of Giles's Kirk!

MCGLASS. At Bannockburn— The Bruce—?

LINDSAY. Sandy: I am in ane spate of words – be silent. Gif
Henry of England, as he plans, as I ken weel he plans, should
turn his calculation, sir, towart ane second Flodden – King
James bean young and oer-tormentit by a wheen sorry
intriguers at his Court – whaur will then reside the protection
for our people?

GILNOCKIE. Here.

LINDSAY (*walking round each of the* ARMSTRONGS). Here . . .
here: here: here. And the King is conscious of it, sir, and for
that reason he doth pray you pardon his prior intransigence
against the valour of your clan. He has sent me to tell you
that gif you will render him ane true and leal obedience
hencefurth, he will put his Royal trust in you, and look to
you and yours to keep his historic Crown for ever integrate,
and Scots! There is ane specific offer—

GILNOCKIE. Specific: aye.

LINDSAY. Ane specific offer of Royal privilege I am commandit to present to ye. I will ask Mr Alexander to expound
it now – he is weel versit indeed in the legalities and practi-
calities. Sandy?

MCGLASS. The King's offer is maist bountiful, ane preclair,
majestical, and unprecedentit offer – I hope ye will agree.
Upon receipt of ane true assurance frae John, Laird of
Gilnockie, that he will follow the course of war ahint nae
other banner than that of King James of Scotland, King
James has determinit to create and dispone for him ane
office of mickle dignity and honour: to wit, Warden of
Eskdale and Free Lieutenant of the King; permitten the said
John, upon occasion of fray, the sole right and privilege
within Eskdale, Liddesdale, and Teviotdale, of defence,
command, and levy. I wad add to that, forbye, that ony

passage of theft across the borders of England in time of peace or truce is maist strictly to be renouncit. Renunciation receivit, King James will then rescind the decrees of outlawry and rebellion heretofore postit against John of Gilnockie, and will issue free pardon for all offences committit by the said John or any of his people in time past . . . There ye are!

GILNOCKIE. Nae theft; nae feeden. Then whaur?

FIRST ARMSTRONG. Then whaur, says the Laird, will we obtain our sustenance?

LINDSAY. Ane land unburdenit with the fear of war contains within its ain acres mickle sustenance, and growth of sustenance, Gilnockie: sheep, nolt, swine, fish, fowl of the air, corn upon your hillside fields – and merchants in your towns – ye'll prosper, sir: ye maun attempt it – do ye daur?

GILNOCKIE. Daur? Gilnockie daur a'thing . . . Whaur's auctority?

MCGLASS. Auctority? Aye, sir, we have that. But it's here in my pouch. I canna get at it wi' my hands bandit.

GILNOCKIE. Tam.

The SECOND ARMSTRONG *takes a letter out of* MCGLASS'S *satchel. He gives it to* GILNOCKIE, *who looks at it wisely.*

Seal of the King. Good.

LINDSAY. Will ye no read the letter?

FIRST ARMSTRONG. Do ye think the Laird is ane shave-pate eunuch bible-clerk? Read it yersel.

LINDSAY. Is there naebody here can read? It is writ in good English. Gif I were to read it ye, or Sandy here, ye wad hae but little reason to credit us, I think. Bear in mind we are politicians.

GILNOCKIE'S WIFE. I can read the letter.

LINDSAY. Will ye no let the lady read it to ye, sir? It were best ye should hear it.

GILNOCKIE (*giving the letter to his wife*). Read.

GILNOCKIE'S WIFE. It is ane extraordinair brief letter, Gilnockie.

GILNOCKIE. Read.

GILNOCKIE'S WIFE. It says but these words: 'Sir David Lindsay of the Mount is the King's tongue and the King's ear. Hear him and speak, and the King will baith speak and listen.'

LINDSAY. Precise and laconical. The King has had good tutors in the disposition of his rhetoric. Weel, sir, his ear is herewith presentit you.

GILNOCKIE. Loose.

The men release their wrists.

Warden of Eskdale. Lieutenant. Ane Officer of the King!

LINDSAY. It suits ye exceeden fitly, Gilnockie. Ye seem a larger man for it already.

GILNOCKIE. Maxwell.

LINDSAY. Ah! the Lord Maxwell. Belike ye do suspect that ye wad do wrang to cleave to the King outwith Lord Maxwell's permission – he bean your suzerain, and you in your turn—

GILNOCKIE. Pay him his rents.

LINDSAY. And divide with him your booty?

GILNOCKIE *laughs.*

SECOND ARMSTRONG. When he hears of it.

THIRD ARMSTRONG. Grip the sark frae aff your back, wad Maxwell.

MCGLASS. Do ye hauld him then ungenerous?

GILNOCKIE. Ane mansion-house in Linlithgae. Sups his broo wi' creish Kirk-Prelates. On his chaumer flair is ane carpet. Ane carpet. They did sell it him out of – out of—

THIRD ARMSTRONG. Persia. Wad ye credit that? Ane carpet out of Persia.

FIRST ARMSTRONG. But notwithstanding this: towart Lord Maxwell the Laird has sworn ane ancient lealty.

GILNOCKIE'S WIFE. Aye, aye, lealty. It has to be considerit.

LINDSAY. Gilnockie: for mony years I had care of the King's education. And I did instruct him in a' that was necessair in the government of his realm. Gif he be unable at his present age to compel to his obedience ane lord that lives as saft as do the votaries of Mahomet: God help the kingdom!

GILNOCKIE. Aye, ha ha, God help it . . . Your wame, I heard it nicker.

LINDSAY. Wame? Nicker?

FIRST ARMSTRONG. The Laird wad speir, Sir David, whether or no ye've eaten the day?

LINDSAY. It is maist courteous of the Laird. We havena.

GILNOCKIE'S WIFE. Archie.

The THIRD ARMSTRONG *goes into the Castle.*

The Laird has just come frae his dinner. But meat and drink will be providit ye, Sir David.

GILNOCKIE. Break it with ye. Bread: salt. Ye are the King's Herald: ye bring the offer of the King. Acceptit! I am his Officer. Ye are ane good man. Gilnockie's roof-tree renders welcome. Welcome, sir.

He shakes LINDSAY'S *hand with ceremony.*

Mr Hieland Pen-and-Ink, your hand. Ye are ane good man.

He shakes MCGLASS'S *hand.*

SECOND ARMSTRONG. When ye shake Gilnockie's hand, ye shake the hand of honour, sir.

LINDSAY. Indeed, I am full sensible of it.

The THIRD ARMSTRONG *comes out of the Castle, followed by* GIRLS *carrying trays of food – brown bread and red wine. This is handed to* LINDSAY *and* MCGLASS.

GILNOCKIE *shares it with them in a token but solemn fashion.*

(*To* GILNOCKIE'S WIFE, *who seems disapproving.*) There is ever ane sair question, madam, when a man sees his ancient life upon the brink of complete reversal. Reversal belike of lealty, aye: but of enmity alsweel. (*To* GILNOCKIE.) Maxwell will be your friend yet: and what about Johnstone?

GILNOCKIE (*choking over his refreshment*). What – whilk?

LINDSAY. Whilk? Whilk Johnstone? The Lord or the Laird? I had in mind the baith of them. Ye are at feud with the Laird of Wamphray, and Lord Maxwell is at feud with Lord Johnstone, who is Wamphray's kinsman and suzerain. There is here ane opportunity to put ane end to this sad quarrel; for the Johnstones lang syne hae been the King's servants, while you are now his Officer. Ane meritable wark, the conclusion of truce. Will ye dae it?

GILNOCKIE *laughs.*

FIRST ARMSTRONG (*aside*). What will we tell him, Gilnockie?

SECOND ARMSTRONG (*aside*). Tell him it's made, what else?

FIRST ARMSTRONG. The Laird says it's made. Wamphray is now in condition of peace, with ilk ane of the Armstrangs, and with a' men other. The Laird and himsel hae ridden in amity thegither in pursuit of the wild deer. They were accordit good sport thereat, and they drank as companions upon the side of the fell.

THIRD ARMSTRONG. They claspit their hands forbye as ane true earnest for evermair.

MCGLASS. Is this indeed the truth?

GILNOCKIE. For why nocht? I am ane Christian.

LINDSAY. I'll tell ye nae lie, Gilnockie: this was indeed un-lookit for. Howbeit, it is maist pleisand and agreeable to hear, and God be thankit for it.

GILNOCKIE. Paps o' the Virgin, how delightsome it is to be at peace with auld enemies! Peace! Whaur's my piper? Whaur's music?

FIRST ARMSTRONG. Whaur's reid wine for the gentlemen? The bottle is toom, begod!

SECOND ARMSTRONG. Gilnockie cries for his music.

The THIRD ARMSTRONG *goes and fetches bagpipe.*

GILNOCKIE. Let's hae the bloody piper. Delamont, ye will dance with her. (*Indicates his wife.*) All the maids and men of Armstrang, let them set their feet to it, let them sing and gaily dance!

They dance and sing:

> Oh merry blooms the hawthorne tree
> And merry blooms the brier
> And merry blooms the bracken bush
> Whaur my true-love doth appear:
> He maks his bed and waits therein
> And when I walk beside
> He will rise up like a laverock
> And his arms will open wide—
>
> Oh start up and leap, man:
> And never fall and weep, man:
> Quick quick and rin, man:
> The game will just begin, man—

SCENE EIGHT

[LINDSAY, MCGLASS, GILNOCKIE, *his* WIFE, ARM-STRONGS, GIRLS, EVANGELIST.]

The EVANGELIST *enters from the Forest, carrying a pack on his back. He walks into the middle of the dancers, who fall apart from him and the music stops.*

EVANGELIST. Good people. Scotland is my native realm: but I am ane traveller, I am ane pedlar out of distant lands. In specific, the lands of Germany.

He opens his pack which contains a number of household articles, pots, napkins, wooden trenchers, etc.

And here in my kist I hae brocht hame for your advantage wark of craft and beauty, Almayne wark in wood, clay, claith – paintit and weel-corven, delightsome to your een, ane ornament for humanity, ane gaud for the material body of man. Wha'll buy it, wha'll buy it?

The WOMEN *gather round and look at his goods.*

GILNOCKIE'S WIFE (*taking a Bible out of the bottom of the pack*). What's this?

EVANGELIST. Aye, madam, d'ye look deeper? Why, what is it but ane book?

LINDSAY. Ye'll dae little good wi' books here, master. We live by blood and booty here – it'd serve ye far better to gang to Sanct Andrews.

EVANGELIST. Sanct Andrews, do ye tell me – Sanct Andrews of the Cardinal, the Doctors, the Prelates – this book to Sanct Andrews? Why, they wad cast me incontinent intil the fire of the Inquisitours for this. Brethren, this book is the undisputit Word of God. It is the Haly Scripture, sirs—

LINDSAY. In English?

EVANGELIST. Aye.

LINDSAY. Aha.

GILNOCKIE. English.

SECOND ARMSTRONG. Show it to the Laird.

EVANGELIST. The Laird. You are John Armstrang.

GILNOCKIE. English. Is ane heresy?

LINDSAY. Precise.

GILNOCKIE. Name? The name: Luther? Why?

FIRST ARMSTRONG. He says, for why d'ye bring ane German

heresy here intil Scotland? We ken little about it here, though we hae heard of the man Luther. Expound it. To the Laird.

EVANGELIST. Here, in this forest, they tell me, there are gentlemen that are dividit against their Princes, and brook nocht their commandments. The Prelates of the Kirk are in like manner this day with the Princes of the State. They are forgotten by God because God is forgotten of them. They are outwith His benevolence, for they wadna feed their sheep when their sheep were an-hungerit. John Armstrang – ye are ane mickle hornit ram – are ye weel-fed by your shepherds – spiritual, temporal? I trow nocht. I trow nocht.

LINDSAY. And I trow somewhat different, master. The wame of this Laird nickers nae langer. Why, he is—

GILNOCKIE. I am the King's Officer! God's tripes, I am distendit!

EVANGELIST. Your flesh is distendit. And what of your conscience, sir?

LINDSAY. Aye, what of it? I never yet heard that Martin Luther did enjoin disobedience to the King.

EVANGELIST. Obedience, he doth enjoin, to the commandments of God: and the commandments of God are ane voice that is in ilk ear present. In my puir mortal ear, or in yours, or in—

GILNOCKIE. Here. Set him, here. You are ane heretic. For your conscience, ye wad brenn, in the het fire indeed, courageous?

He smacks the EVANGELIST *in the face.*

EVANGELIST. Struck with the blaws of martyrdom, I yet maintain to you the other cheek, as is commandit me by Jesus Christ. And notwithstanding, bear I furth my testimony.

MCGLASS. There's nae Inquisitour whatever upon these borders here. Ye maun send him awa north to the correct process of the Kirk – will ye do that for him, Gilnockie, and manifest in public your true responsibility to this Christian Kingdom?

GILNOCKIE'S WIFE. To see him brennt in agony for nocht but his conscience; it wad be ane unco cruelty.

GILNOCKIE. Aye, cruelty. Delamont: *his* conscience: *mine:* what about *yours*?

LINDSAY. Wad ye speir my opinion, Mr Lieutenant? I'm nae ecclesiast. But see, this good man, he is but, as he saith, ane pedlar, his merchandise is tawdry, the wark of some Almayne boor, it's naething at a' – we mak pots as good as this in Scotland. The book alane is notable. Master, I will purchase this, I think. (*He takes the Bible and hands over a coin.*) Here ye are – tak it! Now then, Gilnockie, what will ye dae with him?

MCGLASS. Without his book there's nae evidence. Sure ye wad never brenn a man without evidence.

GILNOCKIE. No gien the Lieutenantship to roast mens' flesh for Cardinals. Fidelity, he hath. Fidelity, maist admirable. Godsake, let the carl gang!

The men who have been holding the EVANGELIST *release him, and he gathers up his goods.*

LINDSAY. And hear ye this, Evangelist, as ye tak your good leave of us. Consider what is writ in this book I hae obtainit of ye. I will gie ye ane text to mind – Sanct Paul to the Ephesians, chapter sax, verse five: 'Servants, be obedient to them that are your masters.' For treason, ye will hang. Tak tent on't – ye will.

EVANGELIST. Aye, Ephesians: same chapter, verse twelve. 'For we wrastle against the rulers of the darkness of this warld, against spiritual wickedness in hie places.' I think ye are ane man that kens weel that wickedness, but by reason of the comfort of your slothful existence, ye wad prefer to oerlook it and thereby to condone it. Within the House of Rimmon is your habitation, and very weel ye may hang me there: but you yoursel will taste damnation. The Lord our God is never moderate.

Exit into the Forest.

LINDSAY. I will now to the King, sir, and inform him furthwith of what has passed betwixt us. I will return in good season and bring you the confirmation of your office. Lieutenant and Warden, John Armstrang, for this time, I bid you fare-weel.

GILNOCKIE'S WIFE. Sir, fare ye weel and may God's grace gang with you. You are ane mild and virtuous envoy.

LINDSAY *gives her the Bible.*

GILNOCKIE. Salutation – wi' your bonnets aff, stand!

The MEN *line up bareheaded.*
The WOMEN *curtsey. The* PIPER *plays and leads them all back into the Castle.*

end of Act.

SCENE NINE

[LINDSAY, MCGLASS.]

They walk about the stage.

LINDSAY. Aye, Sandy, salutation. Tak your bonnet aff, stand!

MCGLASS. Did he kill Wamphray with his ain hands?

LINDSAY. Him or ane other. Of course, there is nae proof of it yet.

MCGLASS. Aye, but he will hae done it. And he receives his reward. 'Howbeit', I heard ye say, 'It is ane pleisand and agreeable thing to hear ye are at peace with Wamphray.' Man, what like of peace is ane treacherous murder, for I'll wager it was little else?

LINDSAY. Sandy, ye are gey direct. But it's no the path of wisdom. Now, consider it this fashion: The King set

Wamphray on to kill Armstrang, gif he could. But he couldna, you see, and frae the day it became clear that he couldna, he was nae langer the King's man. Armstrang taks his place, because Armstrang has murderit Wamphray. *Because*, no in spite of!

MCGLASS. And what way do you intend to ensure that this belovit murderer will keep his promises?

LINDSAY. His promises will be broke, Sandy, for Lord Maxwell will encourage it. I believe indeed Lord Maxwell is paid to encourage it by the English Ambassador.

MCGLASS. Unproven.

LINDSAY. Unproven, but gey probable. Though Gilnockie couldna conceivably credit it. The man's ancestors won Bannockburn for God's sake! Single-handit. Did ye never read it in the Chronicles? . . . Now: because our Lord Maxwell is paid by the English to prepare provocation for ane English invasion – *because*, no in spite of – he maun receive ane better bribe than even Armstrang.

MCGLASS. He has a taste for luxury, it seems. What like of bribe wad suit him?

LINDSAY. The destruction of his enemy? Lord Johnstone intil prison: what about that?

MCGLASS. Johnstone is ane leal subject. He is innocent of treason, Sir David.

LINDSAY. It is ane axiom of state that nae Baron is ever innocent. When Lord Johnstone hears of the death of his man Wamphray—

MCGLASS. Unproven.

LINDSAY. Aye, aye, unproven— When he hears of the death he will mak ane feud of vengeance: therefore for the better preservation of the safety of the King and the realm and the—

MCGLASS. Sir: I do nocht like this policy. It is the exaltation of blind flattery and dishonour—

LINDSAY. Blind. We *are* blind: we grope on a rocky road wi' sticks too short to reach our feet. What was it I said:

> To set myself upon ane man alive
> And turn his purposes and utterly win him?

I've no turnit them at all, Sandy. Johnny Armstrang's purposes remain precisely the samen as ever they had been – violent, proud, and abominable selfish.

MCGLASS. He is ane terrible Gogmagog, he is ane wild Cyclops of the mountain: begod he has baith his een – but hauf a tongue in the man's heid . . . Did ye listen to his Gaelic? I think we need to cut his throat.

LINDSAY. Ye ranten feuden Hieland Gallowglass – cut his throat! Cut Armstrang's, cut Eliot's, cut Maxwell's, cut Johnstone's – whaur do we stop? Na, na, but gang ane circuit – indirect, undermine the nobility; and we begin with the furthest distant, Johnstone. Set them a' to wonder what in the de'il's name we're playen at. I think our wee King will enjoy this business, Sandy. He was aye ane devious clever knave in the schoolroom. But no courageous. That's pity. We're at his palace. Blaw your horn.

MCGLASS *blows his bugle at the Palace.*

SCENE TEN

[LINDSAY, MCGLASS, PORTER.]

The PORTER *appears on the roof of the Palace.*

PORTER. Wha is it blaws his trump before King James's yett? Stand whaur ye are and show furth your business.

MCGLASS. Sir David Lindsay of the Mount, Lord Lyon King of Arms, craves ane audience with His Royal Grace upon matter of state and policy.

PORTER. His Grace is at all times attentive to the good services of Lord Lyon. Ye will be admittit upon the instant, sirs.

He descends from the roof.

LINDSAY. We maun dress oursel correctly, Sandy. A robe and a collar of gowd upon us to furnish counsel to the King.

The PORTER *comes out to them carrying* LINDSAY'S *robes of office.*

Aha, here we are: weel attirit for ane work of politic discretion.

He dresses himself.

MCGLASS. Sir David, ye hae forgot.
LINDSAY. Forgot what?
MCGLASS. Forgot the lady.
LINDSAY. Ah na, na. She is in Jeddart, ye tellt me.
MCGLASS. Aye, but she was to proceed to Gilnockie – she will be—
LINDSAY. She will be snug in ane house in Jeddart till we're done here and can send her word. Is the King at his leisure?
PORTER. He is, sir.
LINDSAY. Then we'll enter the presence, Mr McGlass.
MCGLASS. Sir David, at your hand.

They go off into the Palace.

Act Two

[EVANGELIST, MEG, LADY.]

The LADY *comes out of the Forest and walks about a little as though waiting for someone. She wears a travelling-cloak with a hood over her low-cut gown.*

MEG *comes running out of the Forest. She does not see the* LADY, *who withdraws behind a tree.* MEG's *clothes are all ragged and stained and her feet are bare.*

MEG. Whaur is he? Whaur are ye gaen, master? Come here, here. Aye, aye, we're alane here. It is ane richt solitaire place, here. And I will tell you ane secret.

The EVANGELIST *comes out of the Forest after her.*

EVANGELIST. What are ye, woman? Are ye ane gipsy? There are godless gipsies in Scotland in sair need of Jesu Christ, and I mysel am Christ's ain gipsy sent to exalt the sauls of the outcast folk and rebellious men of this forest. What gars ye look at me like that?

MEG. I am in dreid that ye will ravish me.

EVANGELIST. Ravish? Aye, I could. But no the fleshy body. Na, na, the immortal ghaist within it. I carry upon my worthless tongue twa words or three that will maist suddenly arrest and clarify the misconstruction of your life. Now hear this, woman. God did mak man in the image of His glory: therefore ilk ane of us is as it were ane God: but no yet manifest – our flame is as yet hid aneath the warldly bushel of expediency. Ye need nae wealth nor gifts of Princes for to cast it aff. Stand furth upon your ain, and brenn! The gipsies are God's people nae less than are the gentlemen –

let us begin with the gipsies and by the mercy of their conversion gar fire of glory rin thraeout the land—

MEG.

> Glory ? Whatten glory ? I think I will be sick.
> Master, ye carry ane muckle strang stick.
> It was ane stranger than that
> They did drive it far in
> For to harry the life
> Of the black corbie's nest.
> The puir corbie had ane wife.
> For to lig on her bare breist
> Was it her glory or his sin ?
> She kens weel, she kens weel,
> He'll ne'er tread her again.

EVANGELIST. Why, certain you are nae gipsy. I think you maun be gentry. But distractit – forsaken ? And what's this about the corbie ? About bare breists, and – and – glory ? I trow that you did yield yoursel up to ane unchaste lust and now ye feel the torment for it. Is that the truth, ye were concupiscent ! Before we can expound the reformit faith here, we maun pray, woman, pray, for ane deep and grave repentance. Glory – nae glory of foul flesh. Cleanse it first, cleanse it ; there will be nae atonement else—

LADY (*coming forward*). By what ordination of the Kirk are you appointit to be her confessor ?

EVANGELIST (*whirling round*). By nae ordination but by common humanity. I am in dreid for this woman of the conflagrations of Satan.

The LADY'*s cloak has fallen open, revealing her décolletage.*

Aye, and for you, too. Ye bear the appearance of ane frantic courtly vanity. Belike you are yet chaste and Christian : but in these wild woods, madam, the exposition of your secret parts is neither congruent nor godly. Are ye Rahab or Delilah that ye stand thus flamboyant in your lust ?

LADY. Forgie me, sir, indeed. I had nae thocht to provoke you. Though ye seem gey provokable for ane man I had ne'er met till this aye minute. I am upon a journey that went astray in the bad weather, and I seek for the castle of the Armstrangs in Eskdale.

> MEG *gives a sudden cry and backs away, rolling and groaning* 'Armstrang, John Armstrang'. *The* LADY *goes to her and makes some effort to comfort her.*

What ails the lassie?

EVANGELIST. She suffers appropriate pain for her sin, that is all. I wad prefer ye no to speak to her. You are contaminate, like ane filthy honeypot.

MEG.

> John the Armstrang is to the hunten gaen
> Wi' his braid sword at his side
> And there he did meet with a nakit man
> Alane on the green hillside.
> And John John John he killt neither hart nor hind
> At the end of the day he hameward rade
> And never a drap of blood did fall
> Frae the tip of his nakit blade.

They had stroken it instead aboon the lintel of the house of Stobs. And that's whaur I did dwell – ance. But now it is whaurever I can find— Aye, gang ye to the Armstrangs, honeypot, and tell them that ye met me, whaurever. That's the word, is the word, whaurever . . .

> *She runs into the Forest.*

EVANGELIST. I will follow her.

LADY. Aye, I doubt ye will.

EVANGELIST. It is not meet she be without companion.

LADY. I think you are ane lecher.

EVANGELIST. Na, madam, na—

LADY. But ane lecher without carnality. Can ye no see the

improvement of her saul maun wait upon the strength of her
body? What do ye carry in your bottle?

EVANGELIST. Sma' beer.

LADY. Then administer it, with charity. Bring her intil shelter
and look that I hear ye do her nae scaith. I am of import in
this kingdom, master, and I wadna care to see ye brocht
before the Inquisitours. Awa' wi' ye, catch the lassie.

The EVANGELIST *runs off into the Forest after* MEG.

SCENE TWO

[LADY, MAID, FIRST ARMSTRONG.]

The LADY *walks about impatiently.*

LADY. Am I to haver in this forest until the dark comes over
me? Whaur are ye, burd – here!

Enter MAID, *breathless.*

MAID. Your pardon, madam, I had a' but lost my way. The
lave of your people have gane forwart to the castle.

LADY. And nae message left in Jeddart – Sir David, in Jeddart,
he left me nae message?

MAID. Nae word at a', madam. He has travellit direct to the
King, they tell me.

LADY. Then we hae little alternative but to seek Gilnockie's
hospitality. For what it is worth. I doubt it will be barbarous.

They approach the Castle. The FIRST ARMSTRONG *appears
at the gate.*

You are John o' Gilnockie's man?

FIRST ARMSTRONG. Aye.

MAID. We hae come to his castle after Sir David Lindsay.

FIRST ARMSTRONG. He's nae here, but ye may enter. We're
expecten him back within the month. Ye can bide till he

comes. The Laird is hospitable, to the friends of his good friend.

LADY. I thank ye, sir, you are richt courteous.

She goes into the Castle.

FIRST ARMSTRONG. And what's *her* business wi' the King's Herald, hey?

MAID. She wad like fine to dance wi' him.

FIRST ARMSTRONG. Dance?

MAID. D'ye no jig to that like o' music here on the Border?

FIRST ARMSTRONG (*sings*). Och aye—

> She met wi' him in the kitchen
> Wi' the strae strewn on the flair,
> Beside the fire he laid her down
> His fingers in her hair.

MAID (*sings*).

> And first he pu'd the emerauds aff
> And then the diamonds bricht
> That hing upon her lovely halse:
> He didna need their licht!

They both laugh.

FIRST ARMSTRONG. That'll be an action to be seen in Gilnockie's kitchen, I can tell ye – come awa ben, my wee chanten burdie, there's good meat turns on the spit.

They enter the Castle, familiarly.

SCENE THREE Cut

[LORD JOHNSTONE'S SECRETARY, LORD MAXWELL'S SECRETARY.]

LORD JOHNSTONE'S SECRETARY *enters from the Palace.*

LORD JOHNSTONE'S SECRETARY (*to audience*). I am the privy secretair to the Lord Johnstone of Johnstone. Here is ane evil time for all good men of nobility and lineage. My master has been wardit intil the Tolbooth prison at the order of the King: and nae good reason given.

> LORD MAXWELL'S SECRETARY *enters from the Palace and stands by the door.*

That man there – I see him, he sees me – that man there, sirs, is the secretair of Lord Maxwell. Betwixt the houses of Maxwell and of Johnstone there has lang time been feud, but here today is true enormity. Sir!

LORD MAXWELL'S SECRETARY. Good day, sir. Ye are of Johnstone, are ye nocht?

LORD JOHNSTONE'S SECRETARY. As ye weel ken, sir. And you're of Maxwell.

LORD MAXWELL'S SECRETARY. My master commands me to tell ye, sir, that he has great grief at his heart for what has befell the Lord Johnstone this day; it is maist terrible to hear of.

LORD JONSTONE'S SECRETARY. God's Haly Cross, but are ye nocht ane hypocrite? It was at the device of your Lord Maxwell that my master has been wardit; it is bootless to pretend other. Can ye deny, sir, but that there is news frae the Border that Lord Johnstone's vassal and kinsman, Johnstone of Wamphray, rade to the hunten and nocht but his horse cam hame? And what man was it killt him?

LORD MAXWELL'S SECRETARY. Belike ane Armstrang or ane Eliot. He was at feud with baith of them, it matters little whilk.

LORD JOHNSTONE'S SECRETARY. Ye do admit it?

LORD MAXWELL'S SECRETARY. Why nocht? It is apparent. But ye do Lord Maxwell wrang, to credit that he condones sic murder at the hands of his vassals.

LORD JOHNSTONE'S SECRETARY. Then why is my Lord in the Tolbooth? Because the King has determinit, by the advice of David Lindsay, to concede to Johnny Armstrang a'thing that he demands: and that includes protection frae the just vengeancy of the Johnstones anent his wicked murder. Armstrang is Maxwell's man: and there is occult collusion here betwixt Lindsay and Maxwell. Maxwell craves ane absolute auctority ower every laird upon the South-West Border—

LORD MAXWELL'S SECRETARY. And what does Lindsay crave?

LORD JOHNSTONE'S SECRETARY. Aye, ane good question. I have nae clearness whatever about the motivations of Lindsay.

LORD MAXWELL'S SECRETARY. And neither has Lord Maxwell. Lindsay has persuadit His Royal Grace that your master is a danger to the kingdom.

LORD JOHNSTONE'S SECRETARY. I had rather say a danger to the Armstrangs.

LORD MAXWELL'S SECRETARY. Ah. Ye havena heard?

LORD JOHNSTONE'S SECRETARY. Heard what?

LORD MAXWELL'S SECRETARY. Why, man, the Armstrangs *are* the kingdom! Lindsay has had Gilnockie made Lieutenant of the Border and sole Warden of Eskdale!

LORD JOHNSTONE'S SECRETARY. He has had him made—

LORD MAXWELL'S SECRETARY. Aye! He is an Officer, ane Officer of sae strang ane title that it rins directly counter, sir, to the hereditary privileges of Maxwell his Lord.

LORD JOHNSTONE'S SECRETARY. But – but what is Lindsay's purpose, sir, what d'ye think can be his—

SCENE FOUR

[LORD JOHNSTONE'S SECRETARY, LORD MAXWELL'S SECRETARY, *the* CARDINAL'S SECRETARY.]

The CARDINAL'S SECRETARY *enters from the Palace. He is a Dominican Friar.*

CARDINAL'S SECRETARY. I will expound to ye his purpose, gentlemen. The Blessen of God be upon ye baith, and the Haly Sancts of Heaven assist your deliberations. I represent the Cardinal Archbishop of Sanct Andrews. I will declare to ye for your recollection some portion of that severe and solemn curse late set by His Grace the Archbishop of Glasgow upon the common traitors and thieves that wad break the peace of the Border. The Lord Archbishop said: 'I curse their heid and all the hairs of their heid: I curse their face, their een, their mouth, their neise, their tongue, their teeth, their crag, their shoulders, their breist, their heart, their wame, before and behind, within and without. I curse them gangen, I curse them riden, I curse them standen, I curse them sitten, and finally I condemn them perpetually to the deep pit of hell, there to remain, with Lucifeir and all his fellows.' For of necessity, gentlemen, peace between Christian realms is mair than mere expedience: it is commandit by the Kirk on peril of your salvation. And how, sirs, do we obtain that peace? Assuredly, by maken strang the kingdom, by placen trust in the hereditary Lords that administer the lands upon the marches – your master, sir, and yours: trust that they will refuse all temptation to ride in quest of private booty, trust that they will refrain frae murderous feud baith among themselves and their vassals: and last, but dearest to the hearts of all religious men, trust that they will stand ever ane firm and constant bastion against the spread of devilish heresy.

LORD MAXWELL'S SECRETARY. Heresy, sir?

LORD JOHNSTONE'S SECRETARY. Heresy? Ach, this is plain irrelevance – the man is ane fanatic meddler; let us leave him for God's sake—

CARDINAL'S SECRETARY. Gentlemen, gif ye please! I represent the Cardinal. And I was about to speak of Lindsay.

LORD MAXWELL'S SECRETARY. Aye, sir, what of Lindsay?

CARDINAL'S SECRETARY. First, he is ane adulterer. He hath

ane open paramour. I believe he even sent for her to accompany him on his embassage to the Armstrangs.

LORD JOHNSTONE'S SECRETARY. There is nae man in the Court that hasna had a paramour ae time or anither – why, the King himsel—

CARDINAL'S SECRETARY. Wait. Sir David Lindsay is alsweel ane man of maist remarkable intellect. He is ane clever makar of libidinous poetry, he has writ baith plays and pungent satires: and they are, in great part, contrair the excellence and supremacy of the Kirk. Ye were aware of this?

LORD MAXWELL'S SECRETARY. Of course.

CARDINAL'S SECRETARY. And this is the man the King has sent to safeguard the English Border? What wark does King Henry Tudor pursue within that Border at this present? I will tell ye, sirs: he does defy our Haly Father the Pape – and upon ane matter of adultery forbye.

LORD JOHNSTONE'S SECRETARY. Do ye mean to imply then that Lindsay is ane heretic? Do ye put the name of Luther on him, sir?

CARDINAL'S SECRETARY. Na, na, I wadna speak sae strang as that. Were he indeed ane Luther, the Cardinal wad barely have sufferit his extent the length he has. Na, na, we think he is but moderate. He is nae Luther yet. Likewise we think the King of England is, as yet, nae Luther: but ane sair misguidit bairn of Christ, whose cruel procedures in his realm can some day lead to Luther unless they be preventit.

LORD MAXWELL'S SECRETARY. What ye wad say, I think, sir, is in effect this: ane English aspect of religion and ane Scots aspect of policy are scarce compatible, even in a man of sae subtle a mind as Lindsay.

CARDINAL'S SECRETARY. Scarce compatible. Ane just word for it. Scarce. I wadna put it nearer than that, but—

LORD JOHNSTONE'S SECRETARY. Ye wadna? Then *I* wad. Gif Lindsay is ane heretic, by God he is ane traitor. His intentions are manifest – to mak feeble the defences of the

Border by the irruption of feud and disharmony amangst the noblemen that protect it. Hence Lord Johnstone in the Tolbooth, and after him, Lord Maxwell – whaur? The gallows? There sticks in my mind ane thing alsweel. Flodden. That dolorous field wad ne'er hae been lost had our last King James fand mair support amang his ministers. He had ane flock of faint-heart croakers at his back when he set furth to battle, and Lindsay was their principal.

LORD MAXWELL'S SECRETARY. And James the Fift, his son
. is but ane schoolboy still and still in dreid his umwhile tutor will command him bend his hurdies for the tawse.

LORD JOHNSTONE'S SECRETARY. He maun stand like a man, and stand like a King, with his hinder parts decently coverit, and defer his policy to naebody.

CARDINAL'S SECRETARY. Excepten ever to the Haly Kirk of Christ. Sir David Lindsay, they tell us, is maist zealous in his quality as Lyon King of Arms. Weel, sae that's his function. Let him keep to it.

A trumpet off and cries of 'Long live the King!'

The King gaes to the Abbey Kirk to hear Mass. We had best attend our masters.

LORD JOHNSTONE'S SECRETARY. Attend our masters. For me, I find but small security of employment while this new abundant tyranny of the King obtains towart his barons. Howbeit, sirs, we are agreed upon our policy. Maxwell and Johnstone are nae longer at ane enmity.

He shakes hands with LORD MAXWELL'S SECRETARY.

LORD MAXWELL'S SECRETARY. Ane blessit and Christlike conclusion. What do you say to it, sir?

CARDINAL'S SECRETARY. What should I say? I represent the Cardinal. Amen, therefore, and Benedicite.

    LORD   MAXWELL'S   SECRETARY *and* CARDINAL'S SECRETARY *go off.*

SCENE FIVE *Cut*

[LORD JOHNSTONE'S SECRETARY, LINDSAY, MCGLASS, *the* KING *and* ATTENDANTS.]

LINDSAY *and* MCGLASS *come out of the Palace.*

LORD JOHNSTONE'S SECRETARY. Sir David: Lord Maxwell and my master are nae langer at enmity.

LINDSAY. Hoho? . . . The cause of it nae doubt is the great grief Lord Maxwell feels for the misfortune of Lord Johnstone.

LORD JOHNSTONE'S SECRETARY. They tell me he is maist easily moved to tears for his fellow men in tribulation.

LORD JOHNSTONE'S SECRETARY *goes into Palace.*

LINDSAY. And nae news yet frae Jeddart? God, gif I had her here, I wad set her to lie with Maxwell. For how else can we bribe him now? This means he doth oppose Gilnockie's Lieutenantship. The King is in dreid of him and will undertake what he demands. Gilnockie will repudiate the agreement he has made with us. I think we had best advise the King to put Maxwell intil prison, on the ground of his suspectit intercourse with the English Ambassador, and thereby discredit his honour as a Scot. Sure, after that, Gilnockie wad consider him a'thegither unworthy his continuit obedience.

MCGLASS. Maxwell has ower-mony strang confederates – Bothwell, Buccleuch, the Douglases – the King wad never daur to ward him, Sir David.

LINDSAY. Wad he no? Belike. But we will yet find ane answer. Gif we canna destroy the mickle lords, we maun build up the lesser. As for example, the victor of Bannockburn . . . God, gif I had her here, I wad lie with her this minute. Sandy, we will be late for Mass.

The KING *is carried across the stage in a palanquin. He wears his full regalia and is followed by the* SECRETARIES *from the previous scene (and any other extras available).* LINDSAY *and* MCGLASS *join the procession and exeunt. Cries of* 'Long live the King!'

SCENE SIX

[LADY, MAID.]

LADY *and* MAID *enter from the Castle.*

LADY. And nae word yet frae Lindsay?

MAID. Nane at a', madam.

LADY. And for how long does he expect me to wait his leisure here? It seems that he regards me as his luggage, ane marriet burgess-wife, nae less: and yet he puts upon himself the style of poet.

MAID. He is alsweel ane politician, madam. The King's business is gey exigent and nae doubt requires great courage.

LADY. Impertinent. Ye are forbid to mak mock of his courage, burd. He has that in good measure – it's no his courage, it's his love. I'm nae jimp and rose-wand lassie ony langer – I'm hauf-gate on to be ane auld wrunkled carline, laithsome to the sicht of his een and the caress of his fingers – aye, and the snuff of his nostrils alsweel, I wadna wonder.

MAID. The snuff of his nostrils?

LADY. What else wad ye expect? I hae been dwellen all these weeks in the castle of Gilnockie. I canna describe it as the maist salubrious hall in Scotland. We're a' fair stinkards now, burd: me, you, and every servant I've got left. We're as nasty as the Armstrangs.

MAID. What for will ye no gang back to Edinburgh, madam?

LADY. What for? For David Lindsay, that's what for. Meet me, says he, upon the door-stane of John Armstrang. And

that's whaur I am – and by God I will abide here. Ach, he'll
come back, he'll mind whaur he's left me – he canna dae
without me. When all's told, the chief purpose of the man's
life is naething less than me. Lindsay is ane poet. His lady is
his existence. He has sworn it to me, burd, ane unremittit
aith, wi' the tears upon his cheek-bane.

GILNOCKIE'S WIFE *comes out of the Castle.*

Here's our good hostess. Slender she is, pale, discontentit:
why? She has ane man in her bed like a lion, and eneuch
English beer and beef in her storehouse to fill her as fat as
Potiphar's wife. Good day to ye, lady.

SCENE SEVEN

[LADY, MAID, GILNOCKIE'S WIFE.]

GILNOCKIE'S WIFE. Good day to ye, madam. Hae ye heard
    word yet frae Sir David Lindsay? Is he to come again
    presently to Eskdale?
LADY. Is he indeed? The King's business is gey exigent.
GILNOCKIE'S WIFE. Aye, but the confirmation of Gilnockie's
    title? Gilnockie wad speir gif the title of Lieutenant be truly
    his or no. Sir David gave his promise.
LADY. Then the King will surely keep it for him.
GILNOCKIE'S WIFE. Aye, but ye see, Gilnockie doesna
    entirely trust the King. For why should he? He was five
    times postit rebel: and officers sent against him: he has had
    embargo made upon his land and goods – are you yoursel
    acquent with the King, madam?
LADY. I was weel acquent with his father.
GILNOCKIE'S WIFE. His father?
LADY. Begod I slept in his bed.

GILNOCKIE'S WIFE. His bed? You did that?

LADY. I was but fifteen years auld at the time: but it was a kind of glory for me.

GILNOCKIE'S WIFE. How lang hae ye been the paramour of Lindsay?

LADY. Lang eneuch, madam, for what I've gotten out of it.

GILNOCKIE'S WIFE. He hath ane wife.

LADY. He hath.

GILNOCKIE'S WIFE. And what like of woman is she?

LADY. She did aspire in the warld at the same time that he did. She was ane seamstress of the Court, and obscure – as he too was obscure, bean but ane schoolmaster to the bairns of the nobility. They havena dwelt thegither for ane lang lang time. Sir David had a taste for mair wantonness in a wife than she could provide, and less stateliness of social port. She wad walk like ane Archdeacon up the length of the Canongate frae the palace to the kirk, and she was as dour and rectilinear as the stanes she set her feet on.

MAID. Mickle feet forbye.

LADY. Hauld yer whist, burd: I tellt ye, ye are impertinent.

GILNOCKIE'S WIFE. Madam, amang the ladies of Edinboro and Linlithgow, are there mony like yoursel?

LADY. And how d'ye mean, *like*?

GILNOCKIE'S WIFE. I mean, with nae reck of the vows of marriage – nae shame to be keepit mistress by a man that was weddit in kirk till ane other. I crave your pardon, madam, I intend nae offence. It is indeed strange for us here in the rural places to be told of these things. Gif I were to be fause to Gilnockie, I think that he wad kill me.

LADY. And gif he were fause to you?

GILNOCKIE'S WIFE. Aye, gif he were . . . Whiles, madam, he *is*. But wi' the lasses frae the tenant farms, or the tinker women upon the moss, or when he brenns ane house of the English. He wad never swyve a lady. Haly Peter, it is inconceivable. But you yoursel, madam, you are ane manifest

lady, ye've had ane good education – I doubt you are
capable of baith the Latin and the French—

MAID. Aye – and Greek and Gaelic.

GILNOCKIE'S WIFE. There was a strange man cam hither
thrae the forest, he spak to us of Jesus Christ and the Testa-
ment, and of the New Religions in Germany: how the
priests of our ain Kirk are the foretold Anti-Christ and how
by penitence and martyrdom we can yet again recapture that
liberty of God and of virtue that has lang syne departit frae
the warld. Gilnockie said he was ane heretic: but Sir David
gave him counsel it were better he should loose him and let
him gang.

LADY. I ken the man ye mean.

GILNOCKIE'S WIFE. Madam, it was my opinion that he is
ane godly pastor and he has indeed been grantit ane vision
of divinity.

LADY. Aye – belike, belike, but—

GILNOCKIE'S WIFE. And I trow he would look gey unkindly
upon the adultery you keep with Lindsay Delamont. I will
tell ye this, madam, there was a lassie upon this border, she
lay with a man outwith the bond of wedlock – and what
befell her then?

LADY. What did befall her, madam?

GILNOCKIE'S WIFE. She was casten out by her folk: they
did sparr up their yetts aginst her: and the strength of her
body was broke by the cruel blaws of her father's whip. It
was ane just chastisement: she had brocht shame upon his
house. Forebye the shame was mine alsweel: Her father was
my ain brither, madam.

LADY. What was her name?

GILNOCKIE'S WIFE. She was the dochter of the Laird of
Stobs. And whaur is now the man that had her? I said
whaur is he now? He sprawls beneath a bracken bush and
there will be ane sair vengeance for him yet upon the heid of
Gilnockie because of this murder. Here is Gilnockie.

SCENE EIGHT

[GILNOCKIE, *his* WIFE, LADY, MAID, *the* FIRST ARM-
STRONG.]

Enter GILNOCKIE *from the Castle. He is wearing a new
collar of gold links.*

GILNOCKIE. Murder.

GILNOCKIE'S WIFE. Gilnockie, I didna tell her. I wadna hae
said to her, I wad never hae—

GILNOCKIE. What murder?

LADY. Your good wife, sir, was maintainen her discourse upon
the great respect ye hauld in these parts for the virginity of
your young women. And upon the bitter punition accordit
to the seducers thereof. Is there ocht wrang in that, sir?

GILNOCKIE. Punition no wrang. Aye: bitter. Ye are ane
courteous whoor. Extradinair. Lindsay's. When does he
come?

LADY. That, sir, I canna tell ye.

GILNOCKIE. I should be Officer. Lieutenant! I hae pit up the
title. Had made to me the chain. Whaur's confirmation?

GILNOCKIE'S WIFE. Surely, John, it will be sent soon.
Lindsay is ane trustable man.

GILNOCKIE. Lindsay? To trust him? Ach, he did trust
Johnny. Because that I said I had made peace with Wamphray. Murder. What murder?

LADY. It was but in general talk, sir.

GILNOCKIE (*indicating his wife*). Na. I heard her greet.

He jerks his thumb towards the Castle.

Ben.

GILNOCKIE'S WIFE. Gilnockie.

GILNOCKIE. Ben. Or I'll spin your blood.

GILNOCKIE'S WIFE *goes into the Castle.*

LADY. Sir, you're no wise to be sae ungentle to your wife. She doth love ye, sir, and gif she be timorous it is for your ain safety.

GILNOCKIE. Wha's ungentle? (*To the* MAID.) You. You're wantit within. Willie wants ye.

MAID. I fail to understand ye, sir.

GILNOCKIE. Understand me damn weel. Willie.

The FIRST ARMSTRONG *appears at the Castle gate.*

Tak her ben and steer her. Gif that's what she wants. She has, I guess, sufferit it at your hands hereto – heretofore.

MAID. Gilnockie, I am in attendance here upon my lady. I'm no to be matit at your will to ony man in your service.

GILNOCKIE. Then ye needna be bloody matit. But get out of this place. Willie: I'm on my lane!

FIRST ARMSTRONG. I hear ye, Gilnockie. Come awa, lassie. Sharp. The Laird wad be private.

He takes the MAID *into the Castle.*

SCENE NINE

[GILNOCKIE, LADY.]

GILNOCKIE. Gey private. Tak your claithes aff.

LADY. What?

GILNOCKIE. Here. I want to see your flesh. Aye, and maintain it with infusion of mine. Johnny's the man. They never refuse to Johnny. Tak 'em aff.

She draws a little penknife and points it at him as he tries to embrace her. She is laughing, and he laughs, too, as he disengages himself.

Aha, ha. But you *are* ane whoor?

LADY. I'm no *your* whoor.

GILNOCKIE. But whoor, it is common. Is for a' men. Is for me.

He advances upon her again, more menacingly.

I could. I could violate.

LADY. In your ain castle, Johnny? I belang to the King's Herald: why, man, it wad be treason. And d'ye imagine he wad bring ye the Officership after that?

GILNOCKIE. He wad kill for ye? Lindsay? Mak ane murder? Wad he?

LADY. I canna tell ye that. I've never kent he had cause for it.

GILNOCKIE. For, gif he wad. He is maist honourable. For honour of ane whoor to kill ane gentleman. Honour of ane poet's whoor. Ane Herald-of-the-King's whoor. As ye micht say it, he wad comprehend his obligation. Obligation of honour is the thrust of ane pike, herein, here— (*He touches his heart.*) David Lindsay is ane Herald. He wad therefore comprehend.

LADY. Ah, Johnny, Johnny, my strang and beautiful Johnny, you are observit. And with great disappointment, sir. I trowit that ye had conceivit ane instant desire of love towart me, or lust if nae better, and even lust wad flatter me. You are ane lovely lion to roar and leap, and sure wad rarely gratify all submissive ladies beneath the rampancy of your posture. You are indeed heraldic, sir. Emblazonit braid in flesh and blood, whereas David Lindsay can but do it with pen and pencil upon his slender parchment. I did deny ye your demand this minute because ye were baith rude and rapid: but had ye thereupon attemptit ane mair gradual kindlen of my body, ye micht damn weel hae had me, sir, beneath this very tree.

GILNOCKIE. Aha . . .

LADY. But, Gilnockie. Ye hae been observit. Rude and rapid, aye, but devious alsweel. What ye desirit was never in principle me, it was the proof of the jealousy of Lindsay. For gif Lindsay were to hauld the possession of his paramour,

ane manifest harlot, as matter for gravest honour: then what
way could he condemn you for the murder of – of Wamphray,
is the name? Whilk murder, as I guess, bean to avenge ane
lost chastity. But ye are in dreid it has been discoverit, and
ye willna get your Royal Pardon.

GILNOCKIE. Pardon! John the Armstrang in dreid for ane
Pardon!

LADY. And for why nocht? Ye wadna hae me credit ye attach
sae mickle import to the wearen of a gilt collar and the title of
Lieutenant—

GILNOCKIE. Whist! You mak an abominable roaring with your
mou! Clap it close. Like that.

*He closes her lips with his fingers. He lets them remain there
longer than would seem needful, to which she does not object.
Then he stands back a pace sharply: and unhooks his sword-
belt.*

Here is ane brand. Aff.

He drops belt and sword on the stage.

Here's a gilt collar and ane title. Aff.

He throws his collar down.

Here is ane buft jacket of defence. Aff.

He strips off his buff coat.

Here is my gully. Out.

He pulls his knife out of the top of his trunk-hose and drops it.

I'm in my sark and my breeks wi' nae soldiers, nae horses.
As there were nae soldiers wi' David Lindsay, when he stood
before my yett. Am accoutrit convenient for ane passage of
love. Or for execution. Or for what else? Ane Pardon? Gif
the King himsel were here I wad never beg his Pardon. I wad
demand: bot defence, bot threatenens, bot alliances: I wad

demand he saw me as ane man, that he wad accord me recognition thereas, and that he wad give me as ane man a'thing he could conceive that it were possible I did deserve. And what do I deserve? Ye have ane answer. Speak it. Speak.

LADY. John, ye do deserve to be ane equal man with ony King in Christianity.

GILNOCKIE. In Eskdale. Nae place else. I am maist moderate. I'm nane of your presumptuous Lothian-men, ye ken. Eskdale and Liddesdale alane, that appertain towarts John Armstrang; they are my kingdom, and I content therein my people with the justice of my government. And my government in this small region is ane bastion for the hale of Scotland. The man that strives to pit down Armstrang is the man that means to bring in England, whether his name be Johnstone or Lindsay or even Stuart. They do presume to bribe my honour with their pardons and their titles: and then they do delay – d'ye note – in the fulfilment of their fearful bribes. And they do justify this delay by scandalous talk of unproven murder. They wad gain ane better service out of Armstrang gif they were to cease to demand it as ane service: and instead to request it – d'ye hear the word, request – to request it in humility as ane collaborate act of good friendship and fraternal warmth!

LADY. Why, Johnny, whaur's your lockit tongue? Ye do deliver me these maist clear words as vehement as ane mill-wheel, Johnny. This is the first ae time ye hae been heard to utter without ane weir of tree-trunks across your teeth. And what has causit it, sir?

GILNOCKIE. You.

LADY. Aye, me—
    When I stand in the full direction of your force
    Ye need nae wife nor carl to stand
    Alsweel beside ye and interpret.
    There is in me ane knowledge, potent, secret,

That I can set to rin ane sure concourse
Of bodily and ghaistly strength betwixt the blood
Of me and of the starkest man alive. My speed
Hangs twin with yours: and starts ane double flood:
Will you with me initiate the deed
And saturatit consequence thereof—?
Crack aff with your great club
The barrel-hoops of love
And let it pour
Like the enchantit quern that boils red-herring broo
Until it gars upswim the goodman's table and his door
While all his house and yard and street
Swill reeken, greasy, het, oer-drownit sax-foot fou—
GILNOCKIE. Red-herring broo—
LADY. In the pot. On the fire. All the warm sliden fishes,
Johnny, out of the deep of the sea, guttit and filletit and weel-
rubbit with sharp onion and the rasp of black pepper . . .

*He leads her into the Forest. As they walk he unbuttons and
casts off her mantle, her scarf, and the tire from her head.*

SCENE TEN

[LINDSAY, MAID, MCGLASS.]

LINDSAY *appears on the roof of the Palace.*

LINDSAY. I wad never claim that I had in ony way foreseen or
contrivit this particular development. Gif I had, I wad hae
been ane pandar.

The MAID *comes out of the Castle, humming a tune.*

To the base lusts and deficiencies of humanity. The material
of my craft, in fact. Accept them, mak use of them, for
God's sake enjoy them – here is a wee maid that expresses

her enjoyment in the music of ane sang. She is betrothit to my secretair: she has just been coverit by Armstrang's man: and Armstrang himsel at this moment is coveren— Ach, the deil wi' it!

MAID (*sings*).

> It was upon a day of spring
> Before the leaves were green and fair
> They led me frae my mither's house
> And bad me serve them evermair.
> Beneath the sun that in summer did shine
> And amang the rows of the harvest corn
> The young men took me in their rankit line
> Ilk ane of them of a woman born.

She begins to pick up the various articles of dress and other gear left on the stage by GILNOCKIE *and the* LADY, *and puts them in two piles.*

> Till autumn cam in grief and pain
> And the leaves fell down across the lea:
> There was naething left for me to fulfil,
> But to gather them up maist diligently
> Intil their piles like kirkyard graves –
> The snaws of December, the frost and the gloom
> Will utterly bury them after their pride,
> Deep-buried and frozen, and endit their bloom.

MCGLASS *comes out of the Palace.*

LINDSAY. Mr McGlass, ye maun gang on your lane to Eskdale. I canna leave the Court at this stage of the business.

MCGLASS. Will the King arrest Maxwell?

LINDSAY *shakes his head.*

Your circuit was a yard or twae ower-large belike. A wee King needs but a wee circuit to confine him. We wad dae better to serve the King of England.

LINDSAY. McGlass, ye talk treason.

MCGLASS. Aye. And what am I to talk to Gilnockie?

LINDSAY. Ye are to talk of the increase of Armstrang for the
better reduction of Maxwell. And talk of it with tact. Forget
ye are ane Hielandman. Jacob, Sandy, never Esau – let
Gilnockie be your Esau. God gang with ye.

> LINDSAY *retires*. MCGLASS *comes across the stage to the*
> MAID. *song p 92 a hunting song*

SCENE ELEVEN

[MAID, MCGLASS.]

MCGLASS. *Mo ghaol, Mo ghràdh, mo thasgaidh*[1] – Sir David
sends ye his gallant salutation.

MAID. Belatit.

MCGLASS. Whaur's the lady?

MAID. It is ane question.

MCGLASS (*looking at the piles of clothes*). Aha. She wadna bide
in Jedburgh. There were nae men there sufficient large for
her capacity? Gilnockie's brand. And his coat forbye.
Whaur's his breeks?

MAID. I doubt they are nae langer on his shanks.

MCGLASS. And your shanks? Sin ye arrivit in this place I canna
believe that they've seen nae service as ane saft nakit ladder
for the ascent of some strange venturer? Ah weel, it was to
be expectit, was it no? The King did require Lindsay to win
Gilnockie's purposes – belike the lady will succeed whaur the
politician fails.

MAID. Fails?

MCGLASS. Aye. There is nae office whatever now for the
decoration of John Armstrang – this collar here will signify
him naething while Maxwell and Lindsay stand at ilk side of

[1] My sweet sparrow, my love, my delight.

the King's Grace, aye tuggen at his lugs, left hand and richt hand, till the sacred Crown of Scotland is near to tumble like a – like a ninepin. Howbeit, as I said, maybe, out of this . . . (*He twirls the* LADY's *head-tire in his fingers.*) . . . will we contrive some mair sanguine conclusion. For what reason does she lie with him? For lust, for generosity, for admiration of his strength – or for ane dutiful and politic assistance of Sir David? Gif it were the last—

MAID. Gif it were the last, she were ane true harlot, Sandy, ane prostitute of state: and nae mair worthy of your master's devotion than the bitter wife he had already. My lady is awa with Armstrong because Armstrang is what he is. Gif that be sufficient for her, ye should crave no further reason. Ye decline to speir ower-closely intil *my* behaviour in this castle: it was, ye said – expectit. Let Sir David accord ane equal trust towart her, and she will wark him nae treason. She hath her ain honour.

MCGLASS. As hath Gilnockie. Ha, here be gentlemen.

SCENE TWELVE

[STOBS, YOUNG STOBS, MCGLASS, MAID.]

The two ELIOTS *enter through the Forest. Their hands are on their sword-hilts.*

MCGLASS. Good day to ye, sirs.

STOBS. Good day.

MCGLASS. Ye seek Gilnockie?

YOUNG STOBS. Aye.

MCGLASS. He's no here at the present.

YOUNG STOBS. We'll bide his arrival. What's your name?

MCGLASS. McGlass.

STOBS. Ye are ane Hielandman. A King's rat. I'll put my foot upon ye, ratten. Whae's the burd? She's yours?

MAID. She's naebody's but her ain. Ye have the tongue of a
carl and ane auld carl forbye. Learn some courtesy, gif ye
can; ye are dressit like a gentleman, but your manners are
scarce concomitant.

STOBS. They are the manners of the country, lassie, and the
country's no yours. Sae adapt yoursel with speed, or else
haud your whist.

YOUNG STOBS. Will I clap her across the mou and haud it
for her, father?

STOBS. Ye will nocht. We are within Gilnockie's boundaries
and we'll leave her to him.

YOUNG STOBS. Frae what I hear, Gilnockie's dislike of
vermin in his house is no sae strang as it used to be.

STOBS. That's eneuch o' that, boy. Gilnockie is wed to my
sister. He has benefit of our good opinion until sic time as
it is proven misplacit. When does the Laird come back? I'm
talking to you!

MCGLASS. I'm no in his confidence. He will be back when he
comes.

MAID. He will be back directly, sir . . . he's here.

SCENE THIRTEEN

[GILNOCKIE, LADY, MAID, MCGLASS, STOBS, YOUNG
STOBS.]

GILNOCKIE *and the* LADY *come out of the Forest, walking
amorously, unbraced and dishevelled. When he sees the*
ELIOTS, GILNOCKIE *lets go of her. The* MAID *hands her her
clothes, etc.*

GILNOCKIE. Ah. Gilbert.

STOBS. Aye. It's Gilbert.

GILNOCKIE. Martin. (*To the women.*) Ben the house. I'll call
for ye. You, sir, gang your gate within.

MCGLASS. I will attend you, sir.
LADY (*aside to* MCGLASS). Whaur's Lindsay?
MCGLASS (*aside*). Edinburgh.
LADY. Ah . . .

Exeunt the LADY, *her* MAID, *and* MCGLASS *into the Castle.*

SCENE FOURTEEN

[GILNOCKIE, STOBS, YOUNG STOBS.]

GILNOCKIE. Gilbert—
STOBS. John.
GILNOCKIE. There is ane matter here. Is delicate.
STOBS. Aye. The day we put our blades in Wamphray he did croak ane word towarts me. He said, 'Speir at Johnny Armstrang, what betidit with his honour?' Ye are Lieutenant, are ye no? Ye are King's Warden, are ye no? And what Royal rank, then, is accordit to the Eliots? Can ye gie us the answer to that, Johnny? I wad like fine to hear ye try.
GILNOCKIE. The King of Scotland, Gibby, daurna fecht wi' me. Nor wi' you, neither. He daurna fecht wi' Eskdale: nor Liddesdale: nor Teviot. Is that agreed?
STOBS. Gif James Stuart were to levy war against us, it wad be ane sair war for the realm, and he kens that, aye, his generals ken it, and his captains: his soldiers wadna march. Our castles upon this border are impregnable, and we dwell here, and we hae dwelt, and we will dwell for ay in our ain strang integrity. Therefore, John, what's this?

He has picked up the collar.

Good brother, ye maun justify to me.
YOUNG STOBS. Aye and to me.
STOBS. Martin: I said be silent. Here is matter for the chiefs. Ye maun justify. Can ye dae it?

GILNOCKIE. We grant us then impregnable. But whilk is better: impregnable as ane outlaw – baith back to the Scots and front to the English to fecht? Or as ane friend of Scotland, be impregnable: against English alane? Gibby, we can wear the King's collar. Can tell to the King, we do serve his banner. Are nae subjects, but Officers. Ane like collar for the Eliots alsweel. And yet we fecht the English. Yet we can ride: derive our prey out of England: defend the realm: is glory, Gibby. Is greater glory than here – than hereto – heretofore.

YOUNG STOBS. Nae subjects, but Officers. I canna tell the difference. Ane officer maun obey commandment; when did ye ever hear of ane Eliot that wad obey?

STOBS. At this aye minute: or I'll split your crag, boy. Gif we are the King's Officers, we maun obey him: will he pay for that obedience?

GILNOCKIE. Is possible. Ane honourable pension—

STOBS. Aye. But he may default on it. What when we need mair kye? There's good kye across in England, we canna grip them because of the King's word. But suppose the English were to start ane war themselves? Suppose they were to brenn a goodman's house in Liddesdale? What then?

GILNOCKIE. We can then ride. Defence of the Realm. Ane just reprisal for enormity.

STOBS. Ane English provocation and ane necessair response thereto. The braw Lieutenant levies men, and fills his byres forbye. Martin, expound to the Laird what we have in our mind this day.

YOUNG STOBS. The neist full moon, Gilnockie, it's three nichts beyont the present Sabbath. We can bring ye five and twenty riders— To the south of Carlisle there is a kirk and a wee town o' the name of Salkeld.

GILNOCKIE. Salkeld. I'm no familiar. We will require ane guide.

YOUNG STOBS. We have a rogue at Stobs this minute wad

tell us the Cumberland trackways – aye and conduct us thereacross. Does it seem to you practicable, Gilnockie?

GILNOCKIE. Practicable.

STOBS. Then ye will ride?

GILNOCKIE. Whaur's the provocation?

STOBS. Ah, d'ye hear him, Martin, the Lieutenant has his conscience. Weel: Mickle Sim of the Mains hasna paid me his blackmail this twelvemonth past. So neist week he wakes at midnicht and finds his roof on fire. Wha's brent it? A dozen hoodit riders wi' English badges on their coats: and there's your provocation. Sufficient for ye, Johnny?

GILNOCKIE. Ach, ha: I canna tell. Is delicate. Ane sort of cruelty belike. To brenn a Scotsman's roof, and lay the wyte of it on the English. In time past he has, has Mickle Sim, rade bravely at our backs. Consonant. Can we call it consonant?

STOBS. Consonant wi' what?

GILNOCKIE. With honour, Stobs. There is in this –

He takes hold of the collar.

– ane honour. Howsoe'er we may regard it. Gey delicate. I canna tell.

STOBS. John: we are auld companions, and Janet Eliot is your wife. Stobs and Gilnockie thegither: aye, sin we were bairns. What consonancy of honour was it laid ye in the arms of that harlot of the Court before the barbican of your ain castle, and my sister within it? I did peer with my good steel into the red wame of Wamphray for what he did to my dochter. It is but for ancient friendship alane I hae sparit your life this day. And ye haver with me now upon resumption of that friendship? Ye hae but the ae choice, Johnny: ride wi' the Eliots, or die like a Johnstone. I will in and see my sister: I will mak nae mention in her presence of ony ither woman: and when ye hae decidit, inform me of your will. Ye ca' this matter delicate. Aye, it *is* delicate – it is as delicate indeed as

the hale reputation of your name. Armstrang is ane name I
wad be richt laith to forget.

He and his son enter the Castle.

SCENE FIFTEEN

[GILNOCKIE, MCGLASS.]

GILNOCKIE *stands for a moment, toying with the collar. Then*
MCGLASS *enters on the roof of the Castle. They look at each
other.*

GILNOCKIE. Whaur's Lindsay? He said he wad come back.
That he wad bring me confirmation. I've had made me the
chain. Confirmation: hae ye brocht it?

MCGLASS. I hae brocht ye ane tidings that will emancipate your
joy: Lord Johnstone is in prison.

GILNOCKIE. For what?

MCGLASS. For prevention of feud in pursuance of the death of
Wamphray.

GILNOCKIE. What death? Wha killt him? Wamphray?
When? Obscure, ye are obscure . . . Lord Johnstone to the
black corbies: in the face of Lord Johnstone I spew. Am I
Lieutenant or no!

MCGLASS. No.

GILNOCKIE. Come down here.

MCGLASS *retires from the roof.* GILNOCKIE *puts the collar
on the end of his sword blade. When* MCGLASS *comes out of
the Castle he holds this out at him.*

Young man, will ye tak it. For me, I've nae entitlement. Tak
it: and tak the risk of what gangs with it.

He holds the sword in a threatening manner. MCGLASS *looks
at him nervously, but carefully: walks slowly towards him,*

puts the sword aside and at the same time slides the collar up the blade till it hangs round GILNOCKIE's *wrist.*

MCGLASS. Gilnockie, it's no wise to attempt to be precipitate. There is ane reason for the refusal of the King to accord you this title.

GILNOCKIE. Wamphray?

MCGLASS. Wamphray?

GILNOCKIE. Na?

MCGLASS. Ye hae just said yersel that the matter of Wamphray was – obscure. Let us consider rather the relation betwixt ane vassal laird and his superior. Lord Maxwell is—

GILNOCKIE. Jealous! He is jealous of my merit! He has consortit with the English: there can be nae other explanation. Fornication of the Magdalene, but I will render him ane sufficient cause to feel ane jealousy of me!

MCGLASS. Ye will, sir? And what cause? For Sir David Lindsay alsweel has his merit and his honour struck at in this. Mind ye, he made you his promise—

GILNOCKIE. God, but he did! And he never meant to keep it!

MCGLASS. Sir!

GILNOCKIE. Sir, sir, sir – and whatten wass she cause offence then whateffer to the shentlemen of Rannoch Moor? Tell me for why he has no pit Maxwell intil prison!

MCGLASS. Because Maxwell had ane dangerous faction – there is Bothwell, there is Buccleuch, there is even the Cardinal—

GILNOCKIE. And what about the Hielandmen?

MCGLASS. The Hielandmen?

GILNOCKIE. They are alsweel ane faction, ane bare-leggit bloody faction. Fetch them in.

MCGLASS. I will tell you directly about the Hielandmen, Gilnockie: they combine within their character ane precellent and personal lealty with ane mislike of ignorant insult whether in their ain glens or at the Court, or – na, na, here is Jacob, never Esau, Jacob, Jacob, Jacob . . .

GILNOCKIE. I tell ye, fetch them in, mak ane balance: ane equal – equal—

MCGLASS. Equilibrium? The Hielandmen and Armstrang against the lave of all the Lawlands? Original, indeed, ane new and sophisticate policy: but credit me, Gilnockie, it wad never serve just yet. The Hielandmen are—

GILNOCKIE. Geld the bloody Hielandmen. Pluck aff their sporrans and geld them! I repudiate Lord Maxwell and am his man nae langer. The decision of my conduct, for peace or for war, belangs to me and to nane other!

He calls toward the Castle.

Whaur's that woman?

SCENE SIXTEEN

[GILNOCKIE, *his* WIFE, LADY, MAID, MCGLASS, STOBS, YOUNG STOBS, ARMSTRONGS, GIRLS.]

GILNOCKIE'S WIFE, LADY, *and* MAID *come out of the Castle.*

LADY. Here's three women.

GILNOCKIE. I want the splendid harlot of the Court – you! Ye do speak French?

LADY. I do.

GILNOCKIE. What word in Scots wad ye call Lieutenant?

LADY. Lieutenant – '*Le Lieutenant*' – the man that haulds ane place. As, the place of his master.

GILNOCKIE. Master: is no Maxwell. Master is ane King. And to hauld the King's place craves ane honour of equality. Tell the King his Lieutenant is Armstrang. And as his Lieutenant I demand ane absolute latitude and discretion for my governance of this territory. And tell this alsweel: Johnstone of Wamphray – I do desire reversal of that traitor's property and lands. He did conspire against my life. I am a King's Officer. That's treason. If the lands are no grantit me, ye can tell the King I will grip them!

MCGLASS. But this is enormous, sir: it is inordinate: it is—

GILNOCKIE. It's what I want. Ensure I get it. Awa with ye, the three of ye.

> MCGLASS, *the* LADY, *and her* MAID, *obedient to* GIL-NOCKIE'S *peremptory gesture, retire upstage among the trees. They confer together.*

GILNOCKIE'S WIFE (*brings her husband downstage*). John, ye will never succeed.

GILNOCKIE. No?

GILNOCKIE'S WIFE. The King will never brook it, John. It is too insolent.

GILNOCKIE. Impregnable. I canna understand why I didna tell it to Lindsay at first. Whaur are ye, whaur are ye – Armstrang, Stobs, whaur are ye?

> *The* ELIOTS *come out of the Castle with* ARMSTRONGS *and* GIRLS.
> MCGLASS *and the two women walk out into the Forest. And thence into the Palace.*

Gilbert, the neist full moon. Order your men. Gilnockie and Stobs. Companions. Nae further word and nae need of provocation. Gilbert, we will ride.

> *There is a general cheer.* YOUNG STOBS *kisses the two* GIRLS *in his excitement.* STOBS *grips both of* GILNOCKIE'S *hands in his own. The* FIRST ARMSTRONG *begins to sing, and the others all take it up:*

> Some speaks of Lords, some speaks of Lairds,
> And sic like men of hie degree:
> Of a gentleman I sing a sang

Sometime called Laird of Gilnockie.
He aye wad save his country dear
Frae the Englishman. Nane are sae bauld
While Johnny doth ride on the border-side
Nane of them daur come near his hauld!

Exeunt – the men into the Forest: the women into the Castle.

Act Three

SCENE ONE

[LINDSAY, MCGLASS, LADY, MAID.]

LINDSAY, *still wearing the robe he assumed in Act One, Scene two, is reclining with the* LADY, *and* MCGLASS *with the* MAID, *enjoying the pleasures of love.*[1]

MCGLASS (*improvising verse*).

> This news was brocht to Edinbugh
> Whaur Scotland's King then dwelt
> That John the Armstrang on the border
> His ain state yet upheld.

LADY (*in the same manner*).

> Riever and rebel he was before
> But now ane starker style outsprings:
> He is ane Emperour complete
> Betwixt twa petty Kings.

LINDSAY. Well, ye can baith cap verses with some truth of prosody. It is evident that companionship with the King's makar has to this extent brocht furth its fruit. But for the content of the said verses? Ane Emperour? Hardly that, I think.

LADY. In his ain een he is ane Emperour.

LINDSAY. Aye, and in his ain codpiece, I daur weel hazard. For that's whaur it began. Gif we are at wark upon the improvisation of occasional stanzas, here is ane rhyme of Lindsay's – mark:

> Lady, the love I hae maintaint
> For you nine year—

---

[1] If there is no curtain to provide a discovery here, the characters enter from the Palace.

LADY. Ten.

LINDSAY. For you ten year with nae complaint
                     Should for your treason wax full faint,
                     Maist shamefully expire.
                     But you are ane Ashtaroth of outrage,
                     Ane gowden sepulchre, ane stage
                     Whaur I play out the tale of my gray age
                     Aye for the increase and never the assuage
                     Of venereal desire.

LADY. Jeddart is a weet and a nasty town, David. Ye left me in
     ane tavern there with green wood upon the fire and great gaps
     in the roof. And ye trippit oer the back-ankle of your ain
     metre in the last three lines of your – your—

LINDSAY. Doggerel? It is but doggerel. There's nae astrin-
     gency left. I tell ye, I'm flatulent.

MAID. That's a puir recommendation to my lady of your
     venereal increase, Sir David. I think that ye should—

LINDSAY (*walking about in agitation*). I think I should postpone
     baith venery and poetry and set my wits to wark on policy.
     Lord Maxwell is richt violent angerit against us. The man's
     been repudiate by his vassal. Gif what he will tell the King is
     creditit by the King, there will be ane rope around this
     halse in less than two weeks.

MCGLASS. Ane noosit rope, lady. This is nae game.

MAID. Sandy, we ken that.

MCGLASS. Aye? But to her it *was* game. She did embolden
     John Armstrang to the extent they will impeach Lindsay!

LADY. Mr Alexander, the King will never credit Maxwell. The
     King hates Maxwell. He will require his Lindsay yet, the
     man that did divert his puberty nocht alane with the Latin
     Grammar, but alsweel with the bawdy satires of Petronius.
     My misbehaviour ye did satirize as the wark of ane Ashtaroth
     – ane carnal goddess, David – then accept the goddess's gift
     and build your policy upon it. To begin: surely Maxwell
     repudiate is ane benefit to the realm?

LINDSAY. Ane benefit to the Lairds on yon side of the English
Border. John of Gilnockie, with nae suzerain to control
him, wad be ane honest man to deal with, wad he no? For
his treacheries derive frae the occult procuration of dark men
that movit ahint of him: and they're gane. Sandy – what's
the adage: 'The English of the North and the Border Scot'?

MCGLASS.

The English of the North and the Border Scot
Are ilk ane like the ither:
Their tongue is the same and their life is the same
Ilk man is as puir as his brither.

LINDSAY. Precise. Now: ane free confederacy of the borderers
of either nation, ane alliance of mutual poverty, with their
ain Parliament, gif ye will, under the leadership of – why
nocht Armstrang? In the manner of the mountain cantons of
the Switzers as I hae observit them on my travels. Nae
hereditaire nobility, nae theft, nae feuden, and gif they lust
yet for battle – ane mercenary service in the army of the
Pape, or the Emperour, or the King of France. What's
wrang wi' it?

MAID. England.

MCGLASS. It is ridiculous and unpractical. England wad never
consent to it – why, it wad mean peace!

LINDSAY. King Henry has preoccupations. Religious, finan-
cial, amorous. I trow that he craves for peace – sincerely.

MCGLASS. He craves for the execution of Gilnockie and I think
that we hae nae choice but to gie it him.

LINDSAY. What way, man? Whaur's your army, whae's your
hangman – you? Wad ye mak your name ane byword for
tyranny and coercion, and – and—

LADY. David, recollect yoursel – ye hae the reputation of ane
man of placidity.

LINDSAY. Mak me placid, then. Love me.

She does so.

McGlass, what I hae tellt ye is practicable, and it is honourable. I hae writ indeed ane letter about it – ane treasonable letter, to the English Ambassador.

LADY. David, that is dangerous!

LINDSAY. Agreeable danger. I did ever tak pleasure in ane devious activity. God help me, I'm as bad as Maxwell.

SCENE TWO

[LINDSAY, MCGLASS, LADY, MAID, *the three* SECRETARIES.]

The three SECRETARIES *enter from the Palace.*

LORD MAXWELL'S SECRETARY. What do ye mean, as bad? My master will oerwhelm you yet—

CARDINAL'S SECRETARY. Sir David Lindsay, the Blessen of God upon you, sir; and may He in His inestimable mercy oerlook your transgressions.

LINDSAY. What transgressions? Specify. Her, do ye mean? Lady, will ye strip your body, stand up before them like Phryne before the Judges of Athens, and ilk ane of them will return ye ane similar acquittal. Though I doubt they wad expect ye to pay for it in kind. These are gentlemen of commerce – they buy their love and sell it: love of women and love of country. Weel, what's the news?

LORD JOHNSTONE'S SECRETARY. What's the news, the man demands—

LORD MAXWELL'S SECRETARY. Why, ye arrant Machiavell, here is the news—

CARDINAL'S SECRETARY. John the Armstrang, Thomas his brother, the Eliots of Stobs, and other of their gang, hae ridden intil Cumberland. The town of Salkeld is brennt. The Laird of Salkeld is slain within his ain fold-yard: and the Lord Warden at Carlisle has ordainit ane general muster of his levies: for revenge. That, sir, is the news. You and your

slee dalliance amang the heresies of England – ye hae brocht
war upon your native Catholic land!

LINDSAY. And are ye nocht blithe to hear it? Ye smile, the
three of ye smile! By God, I blaw my neise at ye.

He blows his nose at them.

LORD MAXWELL'S SECRETARY. The King will cut your heid
aff.

CARDINAL'S SECRETARY. The Cardinal will brenn ye.

LORD JOHNSTONE'S SECRETARY. Traitor—

CARDINAL'S SECRETARY. Satirist—

LORD MAXWELL'S SECRETARY. Englishman—

CARDINAL'S SECRETARY. There is nae more to say.

The SECRETARIES *go off into the Palace.*

SCENE THREE

[LINDSAY, MCGLASS, LADY, MAID, ENGLISH CLERK.]

LINDSAY. There is a great deal mair forbye. But we maun wait
for it – out of England. Placidity, and patience . . .
Retournons-nous à nos fesses.

LADY. *Mais c'est une situation très grave, mon chéri: il nous
faut penser à notre propre sécurité: pas de fesses et pas de
tétins aujourd'hui – par dieu, c'est terrible!*

LINDSAY. *Non, ce n'est que ridicule – une connerie inévitable,
et c'est une connerie de ton con – tu as tourné le monde entier
tout à fait de haut en bas . . Tais-toi, et baise-moi . . .*
Aha, here he is: I thocht he wad come soon.

Enter the ENGLISH CLERK, *with a letter.*

ENGLISH CLERK. Sir David, we can prevent open war, and
we must prevent it – now. The English Ambassador has sent
me to tell you—

LINDSAY. Did he read my letter yet?

ENGLISH CLERK. He did: I have it here. A very cunning letter, Sir David; you have not even signed it. But nobody could doubt that it came from your hand.

LINDSAY. Absence of doubt is nae presence of proof.

ENGLISH CLERK (*laughs a little*). Your curious proposals, for the establishment of what amounts to an independent sanctuary for outlaws and masterless men between England and Scotland, have been examined with a more sympathetic attention than perhaps you will give credit for. . . . Why not go back to Eskdale and put your ideas to Armstrong? We can do the same to our own rude gentlemen in Cumberland and Northumberland. But we must have assurances that they will remain content within their own boundaries. Your Maxwells and your Douglases will certainly endeavour to stir up disharmony. Will they be controlled, Sir David? This is absolutely cardinal.

LINDSAY. Ach, I canna tell ye: but I'll dae the best I can: creep in and creep out and tangle them whaure'er it's possible. I doubt I'm a wee bit discreditit at the Court here at present.

ENGLISH CLERK. Yes, we have heard so . . .

He goes out.

LINDSAY (*calling after him*). Hey – hey – brenn that letter!

SCENE FOUR

[LINDSAY, MCGLASS, LADY, MAID, PORTER.]

LINDSAY. Aha, they've heard it, have they? Mr McGlass, we maun put it tae the proof. Blaw your horn, we're gangen in.

MCGLASS. Ye'll no be permittit.

LINDSAY. Blaw it.

MCGLASS *blows the bugle. The* PORTER *appears on the Palace roof.*

PORTER. The King's Grace regrets that he is unable this day to find occasion to speak with Lord Lyon.

The PORTER *retires.*

SCENE FIVE

[LINDSAY, MCGLASS, LADY, MAID.]

MCGLASS. Sure it was inevitable that he wad become ane adult.

LINDSAY. God, McGlass, he's nae adult yet. He has acquirit ane different dominie, but he's still *in statu pupillari*. And it is for you and me to pull him out of it this minute. We will accept the advice of our consequential English friend, and gang directly to Eskdale. I intend to bring Gilnockie to a *de facto* truce and handfast with the lairds beyond the border. That includes the Salkeld men: ane strang immediate torniquet before the wound bleeds further. I ken very weel what is in John Armstrang's mind—

MCGLASS. There is naething in his mind but the enjoyment of manslauchter.

LINDSAY. Na, na, the man desires – he yearns in his mirk bowels, Sandy, for ane practicable rational alternative: and I trow we can provide it him. He is ane potential magnificent ruler of his people – he did steer *you* to your muckle pleisure; you tell us what ye think of him!

LADY. Potential, true indeed: but unpredictable, David. Whiles he is generous and intelligent, ane lion, gif ye will – but when he turns intil ane wolf . . . Besides, ye will be rebel; ye will be against your ain King for this.

LINDSAY. Rebel? I am already traitor, it wad seem. Certain it is ane risk. I am about to set ane absolute trust upon King James. This is ane test for him, ane precise temptation: he kens my value, gif he will bethink him: let him see my purposes, and let him see the purposes of Lord Maxwell and the lave: and mak ane clear choice betwixt them. There was a time when his father was your lover. Explain to the son then, what it is I intend.

LADY. I will do what I can, David.

LINDSAY. Gif he be at last ane man, he will discern what David Lindsay means, and then there will be nae mair talk of rebel or of traitor. But gif he prefer to remain for ever the schoolboy that he has been, he will put himself for ever outwith all hope of stringent kingly government. It is ane act of faith to trust him: Sandy, will ye come?

MCGLASS. *Amadain, Tha thu clis is cearr ach tha mise leat agus thig mi.*[1] I will come.

LINDSAY. Ladies, this wark is yours. Begun within the wames of women: now it maun be carryit through, at the hands and brains of men, tormentible, destructible men. Accord us your bitter blessen and get within your doors.

LADY. There are ower-mony brands and lang guns in the forests of Eskdale. Gif ye shouldna return hame—

LINDSAY. Ye may get intil the King's bed. He is of ane age for it, I think.

MCGLASS (*to* MAID). I shall return: in whatever shape they bring me, ye wad never withauld me welcome?

MAID. *Tha thu ro óg airson a'bhàis.*[2]

MCGLASS. *Na creid facal dheth.*[3] Lindsay, are ye ready? Then let's gang: and the de'il gang wi' us, for I doubt that naebody else will.

The women kiss them and go into the Palace.

[1] 'Stupid, impulsive, a miscalculation, but I am your man and I must come.'

[2] 'You are too beautiful to die.'

[3] 'Never believe it.'

SCENE SIX

[LINDSAY, MCGLASS, GILNOCKIE, *his* WIFE, ARMSTRONGS, MEN, GIRLS, EVANGELIST.]

LINDSAY *takes off his robe and puts on a buff coat. He and* MCGLASS *walk across the stage, and call out at the Castle gate.*

LINDSAY. Now then, for Eskdale . . . Gilnockie, are ye there?

MCGLASS. Mr Armstrang!

LINDSAY. Johnny!

GILNOCKIE *comes out of the Forest.*

GILNOCKIE. Here.

LINDSAY. Ah, out of the wynds of the forest, as befits a rank reiver that recks little of King or Baron but uphaulds for a' time the standard of his ain strength. Sir, I do salute you: you are lord entire within your boundaries.

GILNOCKIE. And what are you?

LINDSAY. The salamander of sanity, belike, betwixt the gleeds of your het fire.

The EVANGELIST *and all* GILNOCKIE'S *household come out of the Forest behind him.*

EVANGELIST. Sanity or sanctity, Sir David?

LINDSAY. Ah? Gilnockie, the English are preparen war. I have come to preserve your manhood and your liberty in the face of either nation.

EVANGELIST. You do interrupt with your feckless brawlen the service of the Lord God. The Laird of Gilnockie has declarit himself at last amang the congregation of the Elect. We were about to sing ane haly sang of praise.

He leads them all in a hymn, speaking each line, which is then sung by the congregation:

ALL.   Lord God of Wrath, our arms mak strang
             To deal the right and hale down wrang

             Thy people are but few and faint
             And Thou wilt hear their just complaint.

             Our native land, O Lord doth bleed:
             Assist us to fulfil her need.

             We praise Thee and adore Thy rage:
             Thy words are writ upon our page.

             We praise Thee and adore Thy love:
             O cause, O cause our hearts to move.

EVANGELIST. Again, again, brethren, assail the ears of God!

ALL. O cause, O cause our hearts to move!

The EVANGELIST *launches into an ecstatic homily, while the congregation, moved to excess, interject cries of religious passion.*

EVANGELIST. Let them move indeed, let them pursue Thy impeccable purpose notwithstanding fear and feebleness of spirit—

ALL. We are but few and faint—

EVANGELIST. —until that we can at the last within this barren land of Anti-Christ and corruption declare to the uttermaist—

ALL. Lord, Lord, declare it—

EVANGELIST. —and out of ane hale and sanctifyit mind give furth with pregnant voice the fervent utterance of Thy glory—

ALL. Glory, glory, glory—

EVANGELIST. —and thereupon erect Thy temple—

ALL. Lord, Lord, Thy true resplendent temple—

EVANGELIST. —upon the banks and braes of Eskdale!

ALL (*including* EVANGELIST). Glory, glory, glory, Lord, Lord, whaur is Thy temple?

MCGLASS. And is this what ye want the Lady to tell the King was your intention – to set up ane temple?

LINDSAY. Never.

MCGLASS. It wad hae been better to hae deliverit up this Evangelist to the fires of the Cardinal, as prescribit in the law, and never mind in what tongue is writ the orthodox Gospel.

LINDSAY. Na, na, Alexander – never that neither! God, I am at my wits' end. I had come to maintain Gilnockie by ane argument to his ain self-interest – but this is nae self-interest: this is ane coercive zeal for martyrdom and fanatic excess that I am scarce able to credit.

MCGLASS. Ye trow that our Johnny isna sincere?

LINDSAY. I trow that he isna godly. The man is exceeden politic: mair politic than me. I will ask him ane question.

> *During the above dialogue the drone of devotion has been continuing, but more subdued. Now the* EVANGELIST *cries again in full strength.*

EVANGELIST. For the sins and the errors of our past life, we maun shew furth our sober penitence. John, are ye indeed washit white in the Blood of the Lamb?

GILNOCKIE. White, washit, clean, pure. Glory to God for that I did sin with ane carnal and abominable sin, but glory, glory, glory—

ALL. Glory, glory, glory—

GILNOCKIE. But all is turnit now towart election and salvation—

EVANGELIST. This brand that ye do bear—

GILNOCKIE (*draws sword*). Is the Lord's brand and consecrate—

ALL. Glory, glory, glory—

GILNOCKIE. For the execution of God's enemies and the renovation of His Kingdom!

ALL. Glory, glory, glory. Hallelujah upon Mount Sion . . .
etcetera.

The religious orgasm fades away: GILNOCKIE *comes down to*
LINDSAY.

GILNOCKIE. Delamont, ye are ane vanity. Ye are ane warldly
infection with your collars and vile titles. I am naebody's man
but God's.

LINDSAY (*takes him aside*). There is nae credibility in this,
Johnny, and I think nae practicality—

GILNOCKIE. Ah. Practicality. Hear ye this, Lindsay – your
wee man Evangelist there – ye canna ca' him unpractical.
We intend to extend the Kingdom of Christ—

LINDSAY. Northwarts, or south?

GILNOCKIE. Whilkever direction can ensure me the best
wealth and food for my people. There are monasteries in the
Scots Lawlands. They tell that in Germany Martin Luther
has made free the nuns and monks. And why nocht alsweel
in Scotland? And Johnny will prove ane gey furious
fechter, new-washit as ye see him, white in the Blood of the
Lamb!

SCENE SEVEN

[LINDSAY, MCGLASS, EVANGELIST, GILNOCKIE, *his*
WIFE, ARMSTRONGS, MEG.]

MEG *comes out of the Forest.*

MEG. Lamb's blood or man's blood, it was never white, but
mirk, thick, blue-red, and it dries upon the bleachit linen
stiff as ane parchment.

EVANGELIST. Be silent.

MEG. I wad speak like yoursel the day, master, I wad speak the
prophetic tongue. I was possessit twa year by the fury of

Lucifer: he drave me like a packmare intil the moss and mire of iniquity: in the fleshly beds I did roll and I did wallow.

GILNOCKIE'S WIFE. Haud fast your gapen slot, cousin, ye incontinent wee carline – did ye no hear the good preacher—

MEG. —but there is mair shame than mine craves absolution here. Aye and chastisement forbye. For ane secret murder done on the riggs of the moor – what chastisement for that, master – punition, revenge, ane heavenly correction – I cry, I cry, I cry: Glory, glory, glory, Lord God amend all, strike down the men of blood, strike down Armstrang, strike down Eliot. Glory, glory, Lord—

GILNOCKIE. She's runnen mad—

GILNOCKIE'S WIFE. Ye will no hear her further; she brings scandal upon the conventicle—

GILNOCKIE. It is the fiend speaks within her. Or witchcraft—

GILNOCKIE'S WIFE. Aye, witchcraft—

EVANGELIST. I did trow she wad be penitent . . .

GILNOCKIE. Penitent. *I'm* your penitent here. Wamphray was slain for ane lustful confederacy against me and against the Eliots, and *she* was part of it! Gif she in truth be penitent, God's throat, she should be *glad*! Ben the house, cast her awa, she is ane withcraft adversary – ben!

He leads his WIFE *and people into the Castle.*

SCENE EIGHT

[LINDSAY, MCGLASS, EVANGELIST, MEG.]

MEG (*sings*).

> Fall, Sword of God, upon his heid
> And bite intil his brain
> For he slew the lovely lover of me
> That will ne'er love me again.

EVANGELIST. I did trow that she was penitent.

MCGLASS. Ha, but she is, master. She is your child and your disciple – a wee bit difficult to control, whatever, but yours – observe her, sir, she hath ane strange passion for you. Is it no reciprocate in your ain body? It is indeed, consider: maist certain ye do feel ane risen lust within you! She hath hauld upon your garment – look!

EVANGELIST (*withdrawing his skirts from the kneeling woman*). This is filthy and incomprehensible.

MCGLASS. Then attempt to comprehend it! The cause of her distraction is John Armstrang, that did kill her man. And ye hae sanctifyit that murderer in all verity with the words of the Gospel? Whilk of these twa penitents of yours will ye accept or reject? Ye canna credit the baith of them? They canna be baith guests at the same Christian marriage table.

LINDSAY. McGlass, that's sufficient.

MCGLASS. Na, na—

LINDSAY. It is! Ye will confound all my policy with this fool's talk of marriage tables. McGlass, ye maun tak tent—

MCGLASS. Aye, aye, and gang ane circuit! You put temptation upon the King, very weel – I put it in this minute upon this Evangelist: whaur is conscience and humanity, master – with this tormentit lassie, or with Gilnockie and his brand? Whaur is your conscience – whaur is Christ, this minute!

EVANGELIST. Here, Satan, here—

He snatches the knife out of MCGLASS's *belt and stabs him with it.*

The flesh prevails ever. The Lord hath hid his face. Within three days I could hae biggit the temple in Eskdale. Oh, ye mountains of Gilboa: cover me, cover me frae the abundant wrath of God—

He runs out into the Forest.

MEG. Never forsake me now, master, I will despair; never forsake me, master—

She follows him, crying.

SCENE NINE

[LINDSAY, MCGLASS.]

MCGLASS *has sunk down at the edge of the stage, so that he is half-seated, half-propped against the wall. The knife is still in the wound. He laughs.*

LINDSAY. Sandy, did he wound you? What's sae damn droll, man? Here is nocht but bloody frenzy. Maintain your manly dignity, stand upon your feet – Sandy, do ye hear me?

MCGLASS. Sir David, there is ane gully-knife sticks out at my side. Look. Whaurever we gang now there is ever ane gully-knife, or ane brand, or ane lang rope, Sir David. Nae circuit nae langer: finish it, sir, finish it.

LINDSAY. I will bring ye intil the castle—

MCGLASS. Na, na: finish it. Edinburgh. Finish it.

LINDSAY (*helping him up*). Finish it? Finish it what way?

MCGLASS. The way of the Cyclops, or Gogmagog or whatever. He has deliverit himself, has Johnny, intil the hands of Evangelists: and in the hands of Evangelists there are red reeken gullies. Ye did tak pride in your recognition of the fallibility of man. Recognize your ain, then, Lindsay: ye have ane certain weakness, ye can never accept the gravity of ane other man's violence. For you yourself hae never been grave in the hale of your life!

LINDSAY. That is entirely untrue—

MCGLASS. Na, na, it is utter verity. But John Armstrang is ane gey serious boy: and gif he claims to be ane Luther – he may nocht be sincere in it – but I tell ye, I tell ye, he will be as dangerous – and as lunatic – as the maist promiscuous Evangelist that ever held a book. Now get me intil Edinburgh.

LINDSAY. Ye canna mak the journey in that condition, Sandy—

MCGLASS. I can. Observe me, sir: I'm maken it. Observe, I'm upon the road.

He staggers round the stage, supported by LINDSAY. *As he goes, he sings:*

> O lang was the way and dreary was the way
> And they wept every mile they trod
> And ever he did bear his afflictit comrade dear.
> A heavy and a needless load.
> A heavy and a needless load.

Ye should hae heard me at the first – your rationality and practicality has broke itself to pieces, because ye wad never muster the needful gravity, to gar it stand as strang, as Gilnockie's fury . . . There is naething for you now but to match that same fury, and with reason and intelligence, sae that this time you will win.

LINDSAY. Will win and win damnation.

MCGLASS. Aye, man, ye'll win and be damned . . . Do ye mind what ye said to Gilnockie the first time ye met him? 'There is ever ain sair question when a man sees his ancient life upon the brink of complete reversal!' For my sake, Sir David, will you reverse your life for me? Show to the King the gully in my side: and tell him to act: and first he maun put intil prison: Johnstone – he's there already: Maxwell: Bothwell: Buccleuch: ony man else? I canna mind . . . But let them all be lockit up, upon the same hour, of the same day, and let the King, alane, ken in what prison, they are keepit. Then let him come to the conclusion of Gilnockie . . .

> A heavy and a needless load . . .

SCENE TEN

[MCGLASS, LINDSAY, MAID, LADY, PORTER.]

They have come to the entrance of the Palace. The LADY and the MAID look over the walls and see them: the MAID gives a cry: and they come down and receive them at the doorway.

LADY. David, what's to happen now? Ye wad never kill Gilnockie – David, he was my lover, David—

MAID. Can ye find ane policy to gang ane circuit around this?

LADY. Hauld your tongue, burd: Sir David makes his ain decision here.

LINDSAY. McGlass, ye do disgrace your master. Ye bring the gully in your side for ane nakit witness against me.

MAID. How lang is there left of him of life?

MCGLASS. Burd: I'm a deid man before my dinner. Will ye show it to the King! *Greas ort, greas ort, iarr air an righ Gilnockie a mharbhadh. O mo gheol ghadl bhithinn sona gu bràth na d'aclais.*[1]

LINDSAY. The King will hear me: I will nocht brook prevention. Whaur's his Porter? Whaur?

The PORTER appears on the Palace roof.

The King shall hear me: the King shall see this: the King shall! Let me in!

PORTER. Lord Lyon, please to wait in patience, sir. I will inquire.

He retires from the roof. MEG is keening.

LADY. David, you are ane new man. I am unable to recognize you, David.

LINDSAY (*indicates MCGLASS*). Can ye recognize him?

LADY. I am talken about you. I tellt ye, I am unable.

---

[1] 'Quick, quick, and tell the King to kill Gilnockie. O my lovely girl, I would have lived within your arms for ever.'

The PORTER *beckons them into the Palace.*

Belike the King will fare better. Ye may divert wi' this his manhood as ance ye did his puberty. Indeed, it is provocative of comedy and mirth.

They carry in MCGLASS'S *unconscious body to the Palace.*

SCENE ELEVEN

[GILNOCKIE, *his* WIFE, ARMSTRONGS.]

GILNOCKIE *appears on the roof of the Castle.*

GILNOCKIE. Whaur's he gane? Whaur's the Evangelist? He's no within the Castle – gang out and find him. Whaur did ye leave him?

The ARMSTRONGS *come out of the Castle gate.*

I tell ye, that man, he is the word of Jehovah God, he is the good fortune of Gilnockie, he is the luck of Johnny's house.

GILNOCKIE'S WIFE (*appearing also on the roof*). Be patient, Gilnockie; he will return in his ain good time. Belike he has stayit to pray.

GILNOCKIE. Pray, woman? What? What's it, pray? Find him, bring him in—

The men run into the Forest.

SCENE TWELVE

[LINDSAY, GILNOCKIE, *his* WIFE.]

LINDSAY *comes out of the Palace. He is wearing his herald's tabard, and carries a scroll.*

LINDSAY (*to audience*).
    I did swear a great aith
    I wad wear this coat nae further
    Till Armstrang be brocht
    Intil the King's peace and order.
    To gang against his house
    As ane man against ane man,
    Through craft and through humanity –
    Alas, and mortal vanity,
    We are but back whaur we began.
    A like coat had on the Greekish Emperour
    When he rase up his brand like a butcher's cleaver:
    There was the knot and he did cut it.
    Ane deed of gravity. Wha daur dispute it?

    He walks across the stage to the Castle.

John, I have ane letter. It is ane letter of love frae the hand of the King. Will ye come down and read it? Or will ye let your lady read it? Or will *I* read it, John? I wear my Herald's coat the day: it is ane surety of Royal honour that there will be nae deception.

GILNOCKIE. Read.

LINDSAY (*reading*). 'We, James, by the Grace of God,' and so furth and so furth, 'to our weel-belovit—'

GILNOCKIE. Our weel-belovit subject?

LINDSAY. Subject? Na, na, I canna see it writ here . . . 'To our weel belovit John of Gilnockie,' that's what he says, 'Our weel-belovit John of Gilnockie, Warden and Lieutenant . . . we do hereby send our Royal greeten. We intend to mak ane sportive progress for the improvement of our health and for the pursuit of the wild deer, throughout the lands of the Border. Gif John of Gilnockie, and sae mony of his people as do desire to come with him, will attend our person and household at the place callit Carlanrigg: he may there be assurit of ane richt cordial and fraternal welcome.'

GILNOCKIE. Fraternal?

LINDSAY. Fraternal.

GILNOCKIE. That means he calls me his brither. He wad call King Henry brither?

LINDSAY. Listen to the lave of it. 'This letter will serve the recipient baith as ane Free Pardon and as ane Safe Conduct upon his arrival at Carlanrigg.' The signature 'Jacobus Rex', and the seal appendit. Ye will recognize the seal.

GILNOCKIE'S WIFE. And we are to trust to this letter?

LINDSAY. Safe Conduct, Free Pardon, the King's seal, the Herald's coat upon me? Remember the words of Virgil Mantuan, madam: '*Timeo Danaos et dona ferentes!*' – 'The gifts of your enemies are e'en sweeter to the taste than those of your friends!' The King hath said 'fraternal'. Do ye mean to reject him?

GILNOCKIE. Lord Maxwell?

LINDSAY. He is in prison.

GILNOCKIE. Bothwell?

LINDSAY. In prison.

GILNOCKIE. Buccleuch?

LINDSAY. Prison.

GILNOCKIE. The hale gang of them. I'll no believe it.

LINDSAY. John, ye had best. The King has become ane adult man this day. Ride out, sir, and bid him welcome to your lands. At last, at last, Gilnockie, he has listent to my advice!

GILNOCKIE. It is necessair, this matter should, with earnest deliberation, be embracit.

He and his WIFE *descend from the roof. They come out of the Castle.*

It is necessair, ane good preclair appearance: as in dress, and plumage. Whaur's the men?

GILNOCKIE'S WIFE. Ye sent them to the wood, for the Evangelist.

GILNOCKIE. Evangelist? What's an Evangelist? Call 'em back! Whaur's the women? Armstrang! Armstrang!

SCENE THIRTEEN

[LINDSAY, GILNOCKIE, *his* WIFE, ARMSTRONGS, GIRLS.]

His MEN *reappear from the Forest, and the* GIRLS *come out of the castle.*

GILNOCKIE. The King has callit me brither! My gaudiest garments, ilk ane of them, a' the claiths of gowd and siller, silk apparel, satin, ilk ane I hae grippit in time past out of England. Fetch 'em here.

The GIRLS *bring out a chest which they open and take out rich clothes.*

Lindsay Delamont: tak tent: ye see Gilnockie's putten on his raiment. It is the ceremony: John the Armstrang's pride and state.

He looks at the garments presented him, and strips off his buff coat, and under-tunic.

Here, this yin, that yin – no that, carl's claithing – rags and tatters – that: ane coat of glory for ane glorious King to hauld the hand of his brither! The King has callit me brither!

GILNOCKIE'S WIFE. He did call ye Lieutenant alsweel.

GILNOCKIE. Lieutenant? What's Lieutenant? Forgotten: subordinate, nocht . . . (*He is now dressed in a fine cloth-of-gold tunic and accessories.*) Aha: and now a bonnet.

FIRST ARMSTRONG. The Laird wants his bonnets.

A GIRL *fetches a number of hats.*

GILNOCKIE (*looking through them*). Na, na, for ane cattle-drover, that . . . ane Carlisle bloody burgess, that . . .

belike, but whaur's the feathers? . . . Aha, ye've brocht it.
This did belang to the Lord Warden of the English side; I
dang it aff his heid wi' my fist at the conclusion of ane parley.
Mair of these targets; pin 'em in. (*As an afterthought he puts
on the Lieutenant's collar.*)

FIRST ARMSTRONG. Mair targets, pin 'em in.

*The hat he has selected has a wide brim turned up over the
forehead, with one or two jewelled badges pinned on the
underside. The* GIRLS *now fetch out a box with more badges
in it, and they set to work to add these to the hat.*

GILNOCKIE. On the road to Carlanrigg, Johnny Armstrang
requires his music. Whaur's the piper?

FIRST ARMSTRONG. Whaur's the piper?

THIRD ARMSTRONG (*fetching the pipes*). Whatten air d'ye
want me to play, Gilnockie?

GILNOCKIE. Ane new-made air: I made it mysel': ye havena
blawn it before. It rins in my heid these twa-three days – nae
words to it yet, but they'll come – wait, I'll gie you the line
of the melody.

He hums a tune, carefully.

Can ye follow it?

The PIPER *tries it out.*

THIRD ARMSTRONG. Aye, belike.

GILNOCKIE. Play . . . Set onwards then, we march.

The PIPER *plays the tune, and they start to march about the
stage. They form a little procession, first the* PIPER, *then*
GILNOCKIE, *then the other* ARMSTRONGS, *and* LINDSAY
bringing up the rear. GILNOCKIE *carries his sword drawn,
and holds the scroll, which* LINDSAY *has given him, in his
other hand. His two men carry hunting spears.* GILNOCKIE'S
WIFE *has gone up to the roof of the Castle, and the* GIRLS
have gone inside.

GILNOCKIE'S WIFE (*calling from the roof as they march*). John – John – God send ye safe, John: remember the King is—

GILNOCKIE (*stops briefly to reply*). The King is what? The King's fraternal!

GILNOCKIE'S WIFE. God send ye safe.

She retires from the roof.

SCENE FOURTEEN

[GILNOCKIE,   LINDSAY,   ARMSTRONGS,   HIGHLAND SOLDIERS, *the* KING.]

A HIGHLAND CAPTAIN *comes out from the Forest. He intercepts the procession, with his drawn claymore.*

HIGHLAND CAPTAIN. Stand whaur ye are. Declare your name and business, sir, gif ye please.

GILNOCKIE. Wha's this?

LINDSAY. It is the Captain of the King's Guard. Show him your paper.

GILNOCKIE. Ane draff-black bare-arse Hielandman, the Captain of his Guard – when he rides intil the Lawlands! Hechna hochna hochna hoo – it is a'thegither inconsiderable. Gang past him: blaw your pipe!

More HIGHLAND SOLDIERS *have entered and taken up positions behind the* CAPTAIN.

HIGHLAND CAPTAIN. Sir, I said stand. Gif you be indeed ane gentleman that hath business with the King's Grace, you will have papers thereto anent: and it is to myself that you maun shew them, gif you please.

The KING *is standing among the* SOLDIERS, *but he is inconspicuous in a plain Highland dress.*

GILNOCKIE (*jeering at the* CAPTAIN). Loòk at the legs of him, the puir ignorant cateran – I ken a whin bush in Eskdale that'd wark some damage there, gin ye daur to trample through it!

LINDSAY (*to the* CAPTAIN). Captain MacFadyan, this is Mister John Armstrang of Gilnockie, and here is his Safe Conduct.

> *He takes the scroll from* GILNOCKIE *and gives it to the* CAPTAIN.

KING. *Am bheil fios aige gum feum iad an armachd fhagail an seo? Thu fhein a dh'iarr sin a dheanamh, nach tu, Shir Daibhidh?*[1]

LINDSAY. *Innsidh mise sin dha.*[2]

HIGHLAND CAPTAIN. *Faodaidh tu innse dha cuideachd e nas lugha mhimhodh a nochdadh do Ghaidheil an righ.*[3]

LINDSAY. *O tuigidh e sin an uine gun bhi fada.*[4] It is the King's desire, Gilnockie, that baith you and your men remove your weapons and leave them here.

GILNOCKIE. What? Na—

LINDSAY. Peace, good fellowship, fraternity. Wad ye spite the King's intention?

GILNOCKIE (*to his men*). Aye. Did ye hear him? Spears down, gullies out.

FIRST ARMSTRONG. Dangerous.

GILNOCKIE. Peaceable. Obey it. We are here upon ane trust.

> *The weapons are piled, and one of the* SOLDIERS *carries them away.*

Now then, whaur's the King?

[1] 'Does he know that they must remove their weapons and lay them down here? Your own instructions, Sir David, were they not?'
[2] 'I will tell him, sire.'
[3] 'Perhaps, sir, you would also tell him to restrain himself from insults to the King's Gaelic subjects.'
[4] 'He will understand in good time.'

KING. Sir, I will conduct you to His Grace.

He leads GILNOCKIE *downstage.*

GILNOCKIE. And what are you?

LINDSAY. Ane Officer of his Household, Gilnockie.

KING. Will ye please to come this way.

As they walk across the front of the stage, GILNOCKIE'S
men behind them are silently taken away by the SOLDIERS.

GILNOCKIE. They tell't me it was ane progress of sport,
against the wild deer of the forest. Wherefore soldiers?
Wherefore bloody Ersemen, here?

KING. As it were, ane time of solace and recreation for the
King's dependents: the Border lands are weel notit for the
joy of the chase. Ye wad never wish to withhauld your
hospitality frae men of sic gallantry? Will ye tak a wee dram
with me, Gilnockie, before we see His Grace?

He offers a flask.

GILNOCKIE. Aha, boy, I will that. (*He drinks.*) Ersemen or
Norsemen, Spaniards or heathen English, they're free and
welcome here, every man, every bonny fechter! Gilnockie
bids ye welcome. It's Gilnockie's land: it's no the King's,
mind that. Gilnockie's land and God's. We are reformit,
here, sir: we have ane true religion here; aye, aye, the verity
of the Gospels . . . Whaur's the King?

KING. Aye. Whaur is he?

GILNOCKIE. Hey – what?

KING. There is ane richt curious circumstance, Gilnockie, doth
attend the King of Scotland. When he stands within ane
company, he will be the anely man present wi' a hat on his
heid.

GILNOCKIE. Aye? (*He looks round and realizes that he and the*
KING *alone wear hats. He laughs – a little uncertainly.*) Aye:
nae doubt he will: then it's either you or me, boy.

KING. It's no you, I'll tell ye that! Ye are ane strang traitor.
The hale of your life ye have set at nocht the laws and commandments of the kingdom: ye have made mock of our
person and the Crown and the Throne of Scotland: ye have
embroilit and embranglit us with England the common
enemy: and by dint of malignant faction ye have a' but split
the realm! What in the Name of God gars ye believe I wad
pardon ye now? Gilnockie, ye maun be hangit: furthwith,
direct, nae process of law: our word in this place is sufficient.
Hang him up.

 The KING *turns his back abruptly. The* SOLDIERS *close in
upon* GILNOCKIE.

GILNOCKIE. Hang? Hang me up? But ye sent me ane letter –
ane letter of Safe Conduct—
KING (*without turning round*). Whaur is it then?
GILNOCKIE. Lindsay, I gave it to—
LINDSAY (*deadpan*). What?
GILNOCKIE. Whaur hae ye taken my men? Ane letter.
Delamont. The King's letter. The King's honour, the Royal
seal – but nae man can say a word against *my* honour: the
elect, the godly, me: washit white in the Blood of the Lamb!
Whaur are my men, my leal people? Delamont, they are my
kinsmen. Delamont, d'ye hear me? What hae they done with
my piper?
LINDSAY. What good's your piper now?
GILNOCKIE. For music, what else? Johnny wants his music.
He has fand him words to his new air. Nae piper: nae music:
Johnny maun sing on his lane.

 (*Sings.*)

    To seek het water beneath cauld ice
    Surely it is ane great follie
    I hae socht grace at a graceless face
    And there is nane for my men and me.

KING (*stamping his foot*). I said to you to hang him up. For what do you wait?

> The SOLDIERS *lay hold of* GILNOCKIE *with considerable violence: he struggles: they rip the fine clothes off his back, and wrap ropes around him: they force him on to his knees and drag him with the ropes upstage to the big tree. Throughout this he tries to complete his song.*

GILNOCKIE (*singing*).

> But had I wist ere I cam frae hame
> How thou unkind wadst be to me
> I wad hae keepit the border side
> In spite of all thy men and thee—

> *The words of the song are all broken up in the struggle. They stand him under the tree, throw a rope over the bough, place the noosed end round his neck.*

For God's sake let me finish my sang! I am ane gentleman of land and lineage – and ane Armstrang for ever was the protection of this realm—

> *They hang him.*

cut ?

SCENE FIFTEEN

[LINDSAY, KING, HIGHLAND CAPTAIN, *and* SOLDIERS.]

> *The* KING *picks up* GILNOCKIE'S *coat and hat and other articles of his adornment.*

KING. Will ye look at what the man was wearen? Gif we were to set ane crown upon the carl, he wad be nae less splendid than ourself. The noblemen that we hae wardit intil prison may be releasit upon surety of good behaviour. The good behaviour of Lord Maxwell in particular will carry with it

ane grant of the lands heretofore held by the late Armstrong
of Gilnockie – thereby we may hope to secure his further
lealty to our person. Ane message direct to the English
Ambassador – ye will attend to it, Sir David – recount to
him briefly the course of our Royal justice here at Carlanrigg:
and express our trust in the eternal friendship of King Henry
his master. What mair – can ye think?

LINDSAY. Naething mair, sire. The man is deid, there will be
nae war with England: this year. There will be but small
turbulence upon the Border: this year. And what we hae
done is no likely to be forgotten: this year, the neist year,
and mony year after that. Sire, you are King of Scotland.

KING. We do think we are indeed. Henceforwart, we require
nae tutor, Sir David. But we have ever ane lust for good
makars and faithful heralds. Continue to serve us in either
capacity. Our gratitude is as mickle as our state can contain.
Gentlemen: we will ride to kill the deer.

A horn blows. Exeunt all, save LINDSAY, *into the Forest.*

SCENE SIXTEEN

[LINDSAY, GILNOCKIE'S WIFE, *the* ARMSTRONG GIRLS,
LADY, MAID.]

The LADY *and her* MAID *appear on the roof of the Palace.*
GILNOCKIE'S WIFE *and the* GIRLS *appear on the roof of the
Castle.*

LINDSAY. There was ane trustless tale grew out of this conclusion—

GILNOCKIE'S WIFE. That the tree upon whilk he was hangit
spread neither leaf nor blossom—

LADY. Nor bloom of fruit nor sap within its branches—

LINDSAY. Frae this time furth and for evermair. It did fail and it did wither upon the hill of Carlanrigg, as ane dry exemplar to the warld: here may ye read the varieties of dishonour, and determine in your mind how best ye can avoid whilk ane of them, and when. Remember: King James the Fift, though but seventeen years of age, did become ane adult man, and learnt to rule his kingdom. He had been weel instructit in the necessities of state by that poet that was his tutor.

> *If there is a curtain it falls upon this tableau.*
> *If not,* LINDSAY *concludes his speech with a bow to the audience, and turns away. Other members of the cast immediately re-enter and* GILNOCKIE'S *body is lowered and released before they all make their bows and then exeunt.*

Glossary of old Scots terms

Certain regular usages should be noted:

gh becomes ch: as	'brocht' for 'brought'.
o becomes a: as	'haly' for 'holy'.
ea becomes ei: as	'heid' for 'head'.

also read:

'money' for 'many'.	'no' or 'nocht' for 'not'.
'hae' for 'have'.	awa' for 'away'.
'nae' for 'no'.	'deil' for 'devil', etc.

o (long) becomes ai: as   'baith' for 'both'.

The past tense ends 'it' instead of 'ed' thus: 'defendit' for 'defended'.

'ing' becomes 'en' or 'an' as: 'riden', 'sleepen', etc.

Aboon	Above
Alsweel	As well
Ane	A, An, One
Anent	Concerning
Ben	In
Brand	Sword
Brenn	Burn
Bot	Without
Broo	Soup
Buft	Untanned leather
Burd	Girl
Carl	Person of the lower classes
Complot	Plot
Corbie	Crow (a bird)
Chaumer	Chamber
Crag	Neck
Creish	Fat

Dang	Knocked (past tense)
Daur	Dare
Dominie	Schoolmaster
Draff	Rubbish (a technical term from brewing, I think)
Dram	Drink
Eneuch	Enough
Erse	Gaelic
Fecht	Fight
Flair	Floor
Forbye	Moreover
Fou	Drunk (literally, Full)
Gate	Way
Gat-leggit	With legs outspread
Gey	Very
Gif	If
Gleed	Hot coal
Gin	If
Gully	Dagger
Graith	Girth
Greet	Weep
Halse	Neck
Hinnie	Darling (literally, Honey)
Howkit	Hooked
Jeddart	Jedburgh (a town)
Kirkfast	(of a wedding) made in church
Lave	Remainder
Laverock	Skylark
Lealty	Loyalty
Makar	Poet
Mickle	Big
Muckle	Much
Mou	Mouth
Mushrump	Mushroom
Neise	Nose

Nicker	Neigh (like a horse)
Nolt	Cattle
Paddock	Toad
Quern	Hand-mill
Ratten	Rat
Reeken	Smoking
Riever	Thief
Rigg	Ridge
Sackless	Helpless
Sark	Shirt
Slee	Sly
Speir	Ask
Steer	Have sexual intercourse with
Strae	Straw
Swyve	Have sexual intercourse with
Tawse	Strap (used to whip schoolboys)
Target	Jewelled badge in a cap
Thrawn	Twisted
Toom	Empty
Umwhile	Sometime
Usquebaugh	Whisky
Wame	Stomach or Womb
Wean	Child
Weird	Destiny
Wha	Who
Whae ?	Who ?
Wheen	Few
Whilk	Which
Weet	Wet
Whoor	Whore
Wynd	Path or passage
Yett	Gate

Methuens' Modern Plays
EDITED BY JOHN CULLEN
AND GEOFFREY STRACHAN

Paul Ableman	GREEN JULIA
Jean Anouilh	ANTIGONE
	BECKET
	POOR BITOS
	RING ROUND THE MOON
	THE LARK
	THE FIGHTING COCK
	DEAR ANTOINE
	THE DIRECTOR OF THE OPERA
John Arden	SERJEANT MUSGRAVE'S DANCE
	THE WORKHOUSE DONKEY
	ARMSTRONG'S LAST GOODNIGHT
	LEFT-HANDED LIBERTY
	SOLDIER, SOLDIER and other plays
	TWO AUTOBIOGRAPHICAL PLAYS
John Arden and	THE BUSINESS OF GOOD GOVERNMENT
Margaretta d'Arcy	THE ROYAL PARDON
	THE HERO RISES UP
	THE ISLAND OF THE MIGHTY
Ayckbourn, Bowen,	
Brook, Campton, Melly,	
Owen, Pinter, Saunders,	
Weldon	MIXED DOUBLES
Brendan Behan	THE QUARE FELLOW
	THE HOSTAGE
	RICHARD'S CORK LEG
Barry Bermange	NO QUARTER and THE INTERVIEW
Edward Bond	SAVED
	NARROW ROAD TO THE DEEP NORTH
	THE POPE'S WEDDING
	LEAR
	THE SEA
	BINGO
John Bowen	LITTLE BOXES
	THE DISORDERLY WOMEN

Bertolt Brecht	MOTHER COURAGE
	THE CAUCASIAN CHALK CIRCLE
	THE GOOD PERSON OF SZECHWAN
	THE LIFE OF GALILEO
	THE THREEPENNY OPERA
Howard Brenton	THE CHURCHILL PLAY
Howard Brenton and	
David Hare	BRASSNECK
Syd Cheatle	STRAIGHT UP
Shelagh Delaney	A TASTE OF HONEY
	THE LION IN LOVE
Max Frisch	THE FIRE RAISERS
	ANDORRA
Jean Giraudoux	TIGER AT THE GATES
Simon Gray	SPOILED
	BUTLEY
Peter Handke	OFFENDING THE AUDIENCE and
	SELF-ACCUSATION
	KASPAR
	THE RIDE ACROSS LAKE CONSTANCE
	THEY ARE DYING OUT
Heinar Kipphardt	IN THE MATTER OF J. ROBERT
	OPPENHEIMER
Arthur Kopit	INDIANS
Jakov Lind	THE SILVER FOXES ARE DEAD
	and other plays
David Mercer	ON THE EVE OF PUBLICATION
	AFTER HAGGERTY
	FLINT
	THE BANKRUPT and other plays
	DUCK SONG
John Mortimer	THE JUDGE
	FIVE PLAYS
	COME AS YOU ARE
	A VOYAGE ROUND MY FATHER
	COLLABORATORS
Joe Orton	CRIMES OF PASSION
	LOOT
	WHAT THE BUTLER SAW
	FUNERAL GAMES and THE GOOD AND
	FAITHFUL SERVANT
	ENTERTAINING MR SLOANE

Harold Pinter	THE BIRTHDAY PARTY
	THE ROOM and THE DUMB WAITER
	THE CARETAKER
	A SLIGHT ACHE and other plays
	THE COLLECTION and THE LOVER
	THE HOMECOMING
	TEA PARTY and other plays
	LANDSCAPE AND SILENCE
	OLD TIMES
David Selbourne	THE DAMNED
Jean-Paul Sartre	CRIME PASSIONNEL
Wole Soyinka	MADMEN AND SPECIALISTS
	THE JERO PLAYS
Theatre Workshop and	
Charles Chilton	OH WHAT A LOVELY WAR
Boris Vian	THE EMPIRE BUILDERS
Peter Weiss	TROTSKY IN EXILE
Charles Wood	'H'
	VETERANS
Carl Zuckmayer	THE CAPTAIN OF KÖPENICK

THE WORLD'S CLASSICS
ELECTIVE AFFINITIES

JOHANN WOLFGANG VON GOETHE was born in 1749, the son of a well-to-do citizen of Frankfurt. As a young man he studied law and briefly practised as a lawyer, but creative writing was his chief concern. In the early 1770s he was the dominating figure of the German literary revival, his tragic novel *Werther* bringing him international fame.

In 1775 he settled permanently in the small duchy of Weimar where he became a minister of state and director of the court theatre; in 1782 he was ennobled as 'von Goethe'. His journey to Italy in 1786–8 influenced the development of his mature classical style; in the 1790s, he and his younger contemporary Schiller (1759–1805) were the joint architects of Weimar Classicism, the central phase of German literary culture.

Goethe wrote in all the literary *genres* but his interests extended far beyond literature and included a number of scientific subjects. His creative energies never ceased to take new forms and he was still writing original poetry at the age of more than 80. In 1806 he married Christiane Vulpius (1765–1816), having lived with her for eighteen years; they had one surviving son, August (1789–1830). Goethe died in 1832.

DAVID CONSTANTINE is Fellow and Praelector in German at the The Queen's College, Oxford. He has published four collections of poetry and a novel. His academic works include *Early Greek Travellers and the Hellenic Ideal* (Cambridge, 1984) and *Hölderlin* (Oxford, 1988).

THE WORLD'S CLASSICS

JOHANN WOLFGANG VON GOETHE

Elective Affinities
A Novel

*Translated with an Introduction
and Notes by*
DAVID CONSTANTINE

Oxford   New York
OXFORD UNIVERSITY PRESS
1994

Oxford University Press, Walton Street, Oxford OX2 6DP

Oxford New York Toronto
Delhi Bombay Calcutta Madras Karachi
Kuala Lumpur Singapore Hong Kong Tokyo
Nairobi Dar es Salaam Cape Town
Melbourne Auckland Madrid

and associated companies in
Berlin Ibadan

Oxford is a trade mark of Oxford University Press

British Library Cataloguing in Publication Data
Data available

Library of Congress Cataloging in Publication Data
Goethe, Johann Wolfgang von, 1749–1832. [Wahlverwandtschaften. English]
Elective affinities : a novel / Johann Wolfgang von Goethe;
translated with an introduction and notes by David Constantine.
p.   cm.—(The World's classics)
Includes bibliographical references (p.).
I. Constantine, David, 1944– . II. Title. III. Series.
833'.6—dc20 PT2027.W213 1994 93–5741

ISBN 0-19-282861-4

1 3 5 7 9 10 8 6 4 2

Typeset by Pure Tech Corporation, Pondicherry, India
Printed in Great Britain
by BPCC Paperbacks
Aylesbury, Bucks